HARBORING HOPE

D1521862

ALSO BY SUSAN HOOD

Alias Anna: A True Story of Outwitting the Nazis

Lifeboat 12

HARBORING
HOPE

THE TRUE STORY OF
HOW HENNY SINDING HELPED
DENMARK'S JEWS ESCAPE THE NAZIS

SUSAN HOOD

HARPER
An Imprint of HarperCollinsPublishers

Harboring Hope: The True Story of How Henny Sinding
Helped Denmark's Jews Escape the Nazis
Text copyright © 2023 by Susan Hood
Interior and map art © 2023 by the Balbusso Twins
All rights reserved. Printed in the United States of America.
No part of this book may be used or reproduced in any manner
whatsoever without written permission except in the case of
brief quotations embodied in critical articles and reviews. For
information address HarperCollins Children's Books, a division of
HarperCollins Publishers, 195 Broadway, New York, NY 10007.
www.harpercollinschildrens.com

Library of Congress Control Number: 2022943668
ISBN 978-0-06-321448-4

Typography by Carla Weise
23 24 25 26 27 LBC 5 4 3 2 1

First Edition

For Paul, with love

Henny (around age 16–17)

In those times, one climbed to the summit of humanity by simply remaining human.
—NOBEL LAUREATE AND HOLOCAUST SURVIVOR ELIE WIESEL

There is always light, if only we're brave enough to see it; if only we're brave enough to be it.
—INAUGURAL POET AMANDA GORMAN

Denmark caused us more difficulties than anything else.
—NAZI ADOLF EICHMANN AT HIS WAR CRIMES TRIAL IN JERUSALEM, 1961

Whoever saves one life saves the world.
—PARAPHRASED FROM THE TALMUD

AUTHOR'S NOTE

Most of the sources for this book refer to the "rescue" of the Danish Jews. Unless I am referencing a direct quote, book title, or website, I prefer to tell of the "escape" of the Danish Jews. Denmark certainly stepped up to aid its citizens against the Nazis, but the word "rescue" fails to recognize the Jewish people's own efforts to save themselves. They were *not* passive participants but filled with courage, resolve, and resourcefulness in the face of sudden and mortal danger.

WHO'S WHO

Henny and the Sinding family
Henny
Paul, father
Elna ("Chika"), mother
Bente, sister (three years older than Henny)
Carsten, brother (five years younger than Henny)

***Gerda III*'s Crew**
Ejnar Tønnesen, captain
John Hansen, engineer
Otto Andersen, crew
Gerhardt Steffensen, crew

Drogden Lighthouse Keepers
Ejler Haubirk Sr. and his two sons:
Ejler Haubirk Jr. and Ingolf Haubirk

Denmark's Leader
Christian X, king (1912–1947)

Germany's Leader
Adolf Hitler, Nazi Germany's dictator (1933–1945)

German Officers in Nazi-Occupied Denmark
Karl Werner Best, first chief of the Gestapo, the Nazi
secret police, plenipotentiary in charge of Denmark's
civilian affairs
General Hermann von Hanneken, commander in chief
of the Wehrmacht

Holger Danske 2 Resistance Group

Jørgen Kieler, cofounder with Jens Lillelund (code name Finn) and Svend Otto Nielsen (code name John)

Elsebet Kieler, Jørgen's sister

Bente Kieler, Jørgen's sister

Flemming Kieler, Jørgen's brother

Svend Kieler, Jørgen's cousin

Jørgen Jacobsen, a.k.a. Tromle, a law student

Ebba Lund, the Red Cap Girl

Nan Møller, Jørgen's childhood friend

Erik Koch Michelsen ("Mix"), a naval cadet and Henny's boyfriend

Henny Sinding

Mogens Staffeldt, owner of the Nordic Bookstore

Other naval cadets and medical and law students

The Tip-Off Team

Georg Duckwitz, German diplomat in Denmark

Hans Hedtoft, chairman of Denmark's Social Democratic Party

Marcus Melchior, chief rabbi of Copenhagen's Great Synagogue

Among the Escaping Jews

Niels Bohr, nuclear physicist and Nobel Prize winner

Aron Engelhardt

Leo Goldberger

Herbert Pundik

Gerd Lilienfeldt

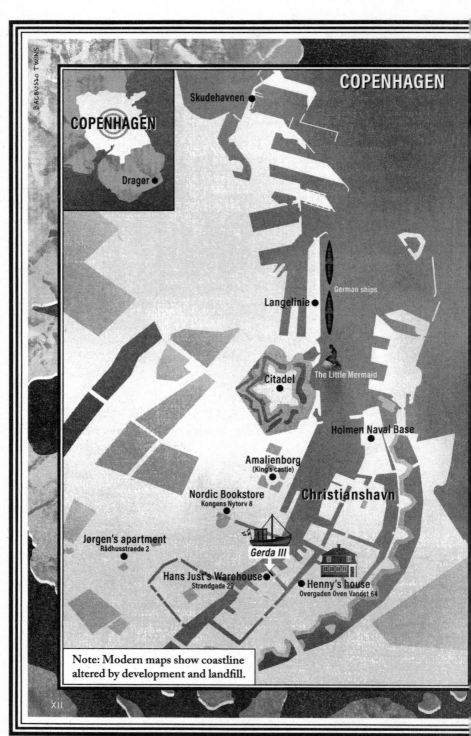

COPENHAGEN

BALBUSSO TWINS

COPENHAGEN

Dragør ●

Skudehavnen ●

German ships

Langelinie ●

The Little Mermaid

Citadel ●

Holmen Naval Base ●

Amalienborg
(King's castle) ●

Christianshavn

Nordic Bookstore
Kongens Nytorv 8 ●

Jørgen's apartment
Rådhusstraede 2 ●

Gerda III

Hans Just's Warehouse ●
Strandgade 29

Henny's house ●
Overgaden Oven Vandet 64

Note: Modern maps show coastline
altered by development and landfill.

NORTH SEA

SWEDEN

Gilleleje

Helsingør

Råå

Barsebäckshamn

DENMARK

COPENHAGEN

Øresund

Malmö

Drogden Lighthouse

Skanör

GERMANY

BALTIC SEA

PART I

Sailor's Delight

SPECIAL DELIVERY

Knock! Knock!
A package at the door!
It was rectangular,
big enough
that Henny had to grasp it
with two hands.
It was addressed to her.
Who was it from?
What was inside?

Henny unwrapped it to find
a shock.
Inside was a gift,
a memento
that meant everything to her—
      childhood,
      family,
      war,
      danger,
      love,
      courage,
      care,
      gratitude.

It was a reminder of all
that had happened.
All that Henny,
her family and friends,
and her country
had lived through,
a reckoning of just
how far they'd come.

It brought Henny back
to the very beginning,
years ago
          to the nights she was on the run. . . .

PART II

Dead Reckoning

BREAKING CURFEW

Henny stole down the dark streets,
leading a young mother
and her child
to the old warehouse
opposite the wharf.
Henny was
just twenty-two years old,
but for days now,
people from infants
to great-grandparents
had been depending on her . . .
for their lives.

Tonight, the young mother
shadowed Henny's every move
while cradling
her sleeping toddler
in her arms.
They had to be as swift and silent
as shooting stars.
Make a wish. Don't tell.
Nazis were everywhere,
even at this hour.
One a.m.

Henny knew it was madness.
If they were caught,
they would be "taken, simply."
They kept their backs
against the walls,
skirting patches of moonlight,
ducking into doorways
whenever they heard
a sound shatter the stillness
of the night air.
Stop!
Wait.
Listen.
Was it wind
whistling through the wharfs?
A cat on the prowl?
Or a Nazi on patrol?
Be still.
Look.
Breathe.

Nothing.
Take a chance.
Go!
One more block.
Turn the corner.

There—
the old warehouse.
Shelter.
Safety.

Henny opened the door
on Strandgade (Strand Street)
slowly, carefully,
hoping it wouldn't creak.
The mother hugged her child
to her chest as she crept inside.
She sighed with relief
as Henny silently closed
the door behind them.
Then she followed Henny
up the stairs to the loft.
Anxious eyes peered
up at them from the shadows.
The mother sat down
among the other Jewish families
quietly cowering
in the corners.
Henny had made this trip
twelve times that night,
guiding one or two people
each time.

There was food and drink
stashed in the hideout
thanks to Henny,
but few had the stomach to eat.
All the small children and babies
had been sedated
so that they wouldn't cry out.
One yowl,
one howl,
and they could all be dead.

ENDLESS HOURS

Time ticked by,
minute by minute,
hour by hour.
Two a.m.,
three,
four,
five.
All through the endless night
the twelve adults waited,
too afraid to sleep.

They were waiting
and watching
for the opportunity
to race across
the cobblestone street
to the wharf
and the twelve-meter lighthouse supply boat—
the *Gerda III*—
that would carry them across the sea,
that would help them stay alive.
It wouldn't be easy,
but they had to try.
It was their only chance to survive.

GUARDS WITH GUNS

Two Nazi soldiers with rifles
patrolled the pier all night.
They marched back and forth
in the dark,
directly in front of *Gerda III*.
Every few minutes,
like clockwork,

the guards met
in front of the wooden workboat,
then turned on their heels
and marched
in opposite directions.
One hundred meters down the docks,
they spun around,
and marched back to the *Gerda*.
Those were the few moments,
when the guards' backs were turned,
that Henny's fugitives
would have to make a break
for the boat.

TIME TO RUN

Just before dawn,
Henny looked out
a warehouse window
watching for a signal
from the *Gerda* crew
on the boat.
There!

Six a.m. It was time.
Tiptoeing down the stairs,
Henny led the families
from the attic
to the ground floor.
Behind a gate
facing the wharf,
she lined them up in a single row.
The boat wasn't far,
just about six meters—
nine or ten running steps.
Her instructions were clear.
Adults would go first;
when they were aboard
Henny would follow,
carrying the sleeping children
one by one to the boat.
There was no time
for discussion,
for arguments,
for pleading.

The guards marched toward the boat,
met,
and turned.
Now!

Henny pushed the first person forward.
He darted to the boat,
trying not to trip on the cobblestones.
The crew lifted him on deck,
and threw him into the hold
just in time.
The guards turned and marched back.

One by one,
Henny cued the next
and the next
and the next person in line.

Parents had to leave
their children behind
and trust that Henny
would reunite them on the boat.
There was no time for fear,
for second thoughts,
for cold feet.
A mother reluctantly
let go of her daughter's hand.
     Run!
A father gave his infant a kiss
on the forehead.
     Go!

When all the adults
were safely aboard,
Henny sprinted across the path
with a sleeping child in her arms.
She or another crew member
delivered each child
one at a time,
each time a potential death sentence
if they were caught.

Henny couldn't think about
that possibility.
She had promised the parents
she would take care of their children.
     And she did.

HIDING IN THE HOLD

Once aboard,
the danger wasn't over.
The crew closed the hatches,
leaving a crack for air,
and the refugees had to wait.

Cramped in the damp hold,
they waited in utter silence—
the silence of a tomb—
until their seven a.m. departure.
Jammed among the barrels
and other cargo below deck,
the escapees held their breath
in a hold designed for fish,
not families.
The dank, stinking space
was no more than three meters by three meters
with about a meter of headroom
in the center of the boat,
sloping down on the sides.
There was barely room to sit
along the sides of the hull
behind the gear.
But it was the only place
a person might hide
if a Nazi guard
peered inside.
The crew piled nautical gear—
tarpaulins, ropes, bumpers, blocks—
on top of the hatch
to discourage searches.
Each thump of the coiled lines,

each thud of the supply crates,
was startling for the families
cowering below.
It was like being buried alive
in the dark, suffocating space.

MORNING'S LIGHT

When the crew fired up the engine,
German guards came running.
They checked the boat's papers
for departure,
as they did each morning.
Gerda's crew had another trick
up their sleeves
to discourage searches.
The friendly Danish men
offered the guards a drink.
Often the guards sat on the top
of the hatch cover
to enjoy their refreshments,
just centimeters from the escapees
frigid with fear below.

The crew and guards joked
and laughed and discussed the weather.
Then the guards moved on to the next boat,
Gerda's crew revved the diesel engine,
and cast off.

Would Henny go too?
No, there were other families
to help that night.
She watched the small vessel
from the warehouse,
watched it chug down
the Christianshavn Canal
to deliver its daily supplies
to the Drogden Lighthouse,
with a secret detour
to drop off its Danish stowaways
to safety on the Swedish shore.

Henny paced a bit,
back and forth,
back and forth,
watching, wondering, wishing.
She knew it was fourteen kilometers
down the canal,
passing under two bridges

lined with German soldiers patrolling;
  another seven kilometers to the channel;
    and then five and a half more kilometers
  to the open sea.

There, the October wind and waves
would pick up.
Then,
it was twenty-eight kilometers
to the town of Skanör in Sweden.

Would the escapees make it
across the choppy waters?
Or would an enemy patrol boat
stop and arrest them?
Or would *Gerda III* hit
one of the underwater mines
the Nazis had moored
to the seafloor?
(At least
the wooden tender
wouldn't trigger
the newer magnetic mines
that blew up steel ships.)

Henny walked back down
the street toward home.

Just a few hours' sleep
to clear her head
and she would begin again:
meet her friends
in the Resistance,
memorize new names
and safe-house addresses
for tonight's escape.

How she wished
she could write things down.
Out of the question.
Too risky.
She'd sleep now,
then steel her courage.
Focus.
Then do it again.
And again.
And again.

Little did Henny know
that in nearly five months' time,
she would be the one
jammed onto a boat,
         sailing for her life. . . .

PART III

Maiden Voyages

CIRCLING BACK TO THE BEGINNING

It was once upon a time,
in a storied land
of kings and queens,
and stone castles worthy
of Shakespearean dramas,
that a sunny-haired,
ocean-eyed girl
was born
to a sailor and his wife.
Not just any sailor—
a navy man.

Henny was born in 1921
as the summer winds whirled
and the blue seas swirled,
encircling Denmark's
more than four hundred islands
just as they did ten centuries ago
when Denmark's Vikings set sail.

Just as they did when Denmark's
Hans Christian Andersen
penned the story of
"The Little Mermaid"
nearly two hundred years ago.

Just as they still do today,
lapping at the bronze statue
of Andersen's Mermaid,
perched on her rocky island
in the harbor of Copenhagen,
the country's capital city.

If you look,
you can see the mermaid's legs
sprouting from her fish tail,
modeling the moment
of becoming human—
a process that can be painful
          and not without its price.

CROWNING GLORY

The land where Henny grew up
was a land of the people,
for the people,
by the people—
its body ruled by democratic elections,
its heart led by a beloved monarch,
much like England.

One of the oldest
constitutions in the world
guaranteed freedom of speech
and freedom of religion.
No single person
could claim all power,
as kings and queens
had in the past,
and dictators
would in the future.
In Denmark,
a solid triangular base—
parliament, government
and the courts—
formed a firm foundation
of the peoples' law,
with beloved King Christian X
as its inspirational leader,
its crowning glory.

But powerful forces
were coming,
forces that would rock
that foundation
to its core.

FAMILY CREW

People often call Denmark
"the Happiest Country in the World."
Henny grew up
content and comfortable,
the middle of three children
raised by
a Royal Danish Navy commander,
Paul Sinding, and his wife, Elna,
nicknamed Chika.

Henny didn't have much time
for her siblings.
Her brother, Carsten,
was five years younger,
so Henny "couldn't be bothered
with him, just a baby."
Her sister, Bente, three years older,
was "boring
because she always did
what she was told."
Henny's family said,

> *Bente was a rather quiet girl, always well
> behaved, whereas Henny was the rebellious
> daughter.*

Neither of Henny's siblings
were interested
in the things Henny did,
then or later.

Henny was closest to her father.
She adored her
upstanding naval-officer dad—
a man as reliable as the
Danish Lighthouse and Buoy Service
he commanded,
as bright and upright
as the Drogden Lighthouse
he supervised,
as strong and steady as *Gerda III*,
the lighthouse workboat
he managed.

HUMBLE BEGINNINGS

The Sinding family
wasn't always so important.
They first lived
in simple naval row housing
named Nyboder (New Barracks)
in Copenhagen.
Dating back to 1631,
these small, sunny row houses
with ocher walls, iron-red shutters,
pine-green doors,
and red tile roofs
formed a phalanx of tiny homes
standing shoulder to shoulder
like soldiers.
Each residence was so narrow,
the garbage collector
had to pass through the kitchen
to pick up the garbage
from the backyard,
near the latrines.
Side by side with their neighbors,
Henny and her family fit snugly
into this tight-knit community
of naval personnel.

MOVING UP

As Henny grew,
her father rose in rank
and with each promotion
came a larger house.
When Henny was a teenager,
Paul Sinding
achieved the rank of commander.
The family
moved to a large, lovely house
in the Christianshavn neighborhood,
a group
of small, charming islands
just a short walk
over a bridge
from the historic heart of the city.
Henny's new street, facing the canal,
was called
Overgaden Oven Vandet—
the "top street above the water."
A top-brass dad,
a top-flight home,
Henny was growing up
on top of the world.

COMPASS

As she got older,
Henny soaked in
her father's
boundless love of the sea
and his unerring sense
of what was right,
what was just.
Her eyes blazed with pride
walking with her father
in his navy uniform.
Her parents drilled into her:

> *Your family name is not an ordinary one.*
> *People will know who we are because your*
> *father is a naval commander.*

It was important
to have a "good inner moral compass,"
but to remain humble.
"One does not boast here in life"
was the family motto.

WORKAROUNDS

Her father knew
he had to live up
to official expectations
befitting his rank in the navy,
but to him,
it wasn't RIGHT or JUST
to spend more money than necessary.
He worked hard to keep expenses low.
Going to official functions,
her father wore
his full dress uniform
accompanied by her mother
in her finest gown.
And yet, they traveled by tram,
switching to a taxi
a few blocks from the event.
Going home, they hailed a cab
for a few blocks back to the tram!

The family agreed in theory
with his thriftiness,
but even their mother
learned to
work around his rules.
Making long-distance calls,

Chika would sneak out
to use a phone booth
on the street.
That way the commander
wouldn't see the expense
on their bill.

Henny learned
from her father
and her mother
that if you were clever,
there were ways
to navigate authority.

DANCING THE DANCE

Henny attended
ballet classes as a girl
with the dream
of being accepted into
the Royal Danish Ballet School.

Her parents wouldn't hear of it,
declaring ballerinas were

"destined to become ladies of pleasure
kept by a wealthy man."
To Henny, that was unjust,
but never mind.
She would find a way
to pursue her passions
of dance and music
while sidestepping
her parents' objections.
She learned to play accordion
and to master the fancy footwork
of step dance.
For Henny,
it was a lively way
to kick up her heels
and stamp her feet!

PIPPI

People later compared Henny to
Pippi Longstocking,
the playful,
unconventional,
compassionate,
"strongest girl in the world"
created by Swedish author
Astrid Lindgren in 1945.
Growing up,
Henny learned to read each situation,
evaluate her options, and trust her gut.
She was not afraid
to oppose authority,
or the father she adored.
Her school for girls—
the N. Zahle's School—
fostered that self-confidence, that spirit.
Founded in 1851
by women's education pioneer
Natalie Zahle,
it promoted women's rights
and welcomed girls of all religions.

HER OWN LITTLE FAITH

Henny was Lutheran,
but her family rarely went to church,
even at Christmas.
Henny had "her own little faith"—
in "something else,
something bigger."
She defended classmates
who were picked on.
Her mother always told her,

> *If somebody comes asking you for help, and*
> *you are in a position to help, then you must*
> *help!*

From first through eleventh grade,
Henny developed
strong, lasting friendships,
especially with one girl
who was in her class all those years—
her best friend, Isse (Annelise) Bruné.

SECRETS (ECRETSINKING)

Early on,
Henny was good at keeping a secret.
"In our family, we do not gossip!"
said her parents.
Henny and her friend Isse
developed a secret language—
"The INKING language."
They would move
the first letter of a word
to the back and then add "inking."
So "secret" became "ecretsinking,"
"school" would be "choolsinking,"
"father," "atherfinking,"
"mother," "otherminking."
At a young age,
Henny was already thinking
like a secret agent.

UP FOR ADVENTURE

Isse's father,
whom Henny called "Uncle Bob,"
introduced both girls
to skiing, skating,
and most importantly, sailing.
As a teenager,
Henny spent hours
racing sailboats
at the Hellerup Sailing Club,
a breeding ground
of world-class sailors
like Paul Elvstrøm,
who took home
four gold medals
in four consecutive
Olympic Games.

Henny took to sailing as happily
as a breeze billows a sail.
Fearless and able
to fend for herself,
she made friends easily,
entertaining the other kids
with her sharp wit

and spirited step dance.
She loved to compete
against boys
and indeed
became a "force of nature"
in everything from dinghies
to nine-meter Dragon sloops
later used in the Olympics.
She caught the eye of one boy
in particular—
Erling Sundø—
but Henny breezed by,
leaving him in her wake.

In winter, she raced iceboats,
keeping the cold at bay
by stuffing newspaper
under her jacket.
She grew to know
the Øresund strait
between Denmark and Sweden
like she knew her own backyard.

That expert knowledge
of the ever-shifting
channels, shoals,

currents, and winds
would serve her well
navigating the perils
of the Nazi occupation
soon to come.

WELL-ROUNDED

"Look after your teeth!"
"Learn languages!"
These were other Sinding family mottoes.
So Henny got braces as a young girl
(not common in those days)
and in 1938,
at age seventeen,
she traveled to England
to work as an au pair
for a British family.

Henny's mother and father
encouraged their children
to learn to
take care of themselves,

see other countries,
learn about other people,
get a well-rounded education.
But only Henny,
their "ever curious
and daring child,"
ventured far from home.

In Britain,
Henny lived another way of life,
learned to speak English
and read English literature.
When she returned to Denmark
in the summer of 1939,
she had a somewhat
broader worldview.

But suddenly,
on September 1, 1939,
that worldview darkened
like an eclipse of the sun.

PART IV

Eclipse

DARK SHADOW

Henny was at home
with her family
when black news
hit the airwaves,
overshadowing everything else.

The Sinding family
huddled together
around the radio
to hear the chilling dispatch.
The British Broadcasting Corporation (BBC)
blasted the report:

> *Germany has invaded Poland and has*
> *bombed many towns. German troops have*
> *crossed all the frontiers.*

Britain and France
went on high alert,
immediately
mobilizing their armed forces.
On September 3,
the British prime minister
addressed his citizens
and the world, saying,

This country is at war with Germany. . . .
[Hitler will never] give up . . . using force
to gain his will. He can only be stopped by
force. We and France are today . . . going
to the aid of Poland, who is so bravely
resisting this wicked and unprovoked
attack on her people.

Henny's thoughts
must have turned
to her young au pair family
and the children
she cared for in Britain,
just across the North Sea.
Would they be safe?
Would the father
be sent off to fight?
And would Denmark
be drawn
into this war?

Denmark had signed
a nonaggression pact
with Germany
just a few months before.
The agreement vowed
"to maintain peace"

between the two countries
"under all circumstances."

Henny's father
listened sternly,
but held his peace.
As a naval commander,
he knew what might happen.

He knew too
that Danes would try to stay
out of the fray,
try to maintain neutrality,
as they had during
World War I.
He knew their government
had pared down the
armed forces over the past decade,
and was ill-equipped to fight.
But he didn't discuss politics.

> *Her father kept things to himself. He*
> *wanted to spare [Henny and the other]*
> *children.*

No one in Denmark,
not Henny, not her father—
no one in the world—
could imagine
the devastating consequences
to come.

World War II had begun.

PART V

Trimming Sails

HENNY GOES TO WORK

Henny took a job
with her father's naval unit—
the Danish Lighthouse
and Buoy Service,
in Copenhagen.
Reporting to an office
down the canal docks
every morning,
she breathed in the salt sea air,
felt the wind in her hair,
watched the water
ripple and sparkle
as seagulls glided overhead.
War seemed a far shore.
And it was the perfect gig
for a girl who was madly in love with
"everything
. . . to do with the sea."

Her work?
Plotting spots for
buoys and lighthouses,
mapping safety routes
for boats big and small.

She took typing
and stenography classes at night
and learned to *tap, tap, tap*
the keyboard
with lightning speed.

At work during the day,
she met a circle of close friends,
the crew of *Gerda III*—
Captain Ejnar Tønnesen,
engineer John Hansen,
Gerhardt Steffensen,
and Otto Andersen.

Though they were at least
ten years older than Henny,
they quickly became friends.

Lighthearted
and quick-witted,
Henny made even
a dreary workday
more cheery.

And she was amused
by these jovial, sunburned sailors

who entertained her with
their harmonicas and accordions
and who peppered their conversations
with salty talk.

Together, day in and day out,
the crew of *Gerda III*
became part of
Henny's extended family,
bonded by the ties
of common work,
witty repartee,
lively music,
and a love of the water.

LIFEBOAT

Gerda III was a common workboat
built in 1926 of simple stuff—
twelve meters
of pine and oak,
four meters wide,
two meters deep,
with a small cabin for crew,
a hold for fish,
a few small steadying sails,
powered by
a "semi-diesel" engine.

Estimated cruising speed?
Eight knots,
about fifteen kilometers per hour.
Not fast, but strong,
hardy enough to weather
the weltering wind and waves
of the wild Øresund sea.

The trusty craft set off each morning,
proudly flying its small Danish flag,
on an ordinary, but essential mission:
to deliver food and supplies,

mail, books, and newspapers,
to the lighthouse keepers
at Drogden Light.

Gerda III also serviced and maintained
the buoys in the Øresund,
buoys that guided all the national
and international ships traveling
between the Baltic and North Seas.
She was a lookout, a caretaker,
an emissary of goodwill
on the high seas.

The boat cast off each morning
and returned to the dock each night,
a circuit as ordinary and predictable
as the ebbing and flowing tide,
as the waxing and waning moon.

Despite her modest appearance
and everyday routine,
Gerda III was as essential as air
to those who depended on her—
the lighthouse keepers
of Drogden Light.

No one knew that, in time,
this humble workboat
would be recast
as an ark,
a lifeboat,
a vessel of goodness and grace,
that would mean survival
for so many.

One
scarlet light
in a lantern room
with a one-thousand-
watt bulb flashed three
times every fifteen
seconds, lighting the dark
more than thirty
kilometers away.

Below: a stout boxy
block of a building
painted in broad stripes,
red and white—a keeper's
cottage to a father and

two sons with a radio, books,
charts, cozy armchairs, a kitchen,
several bedrooms, and bathrooms.

The men watched the weather, tested
the waters, registered the hundreds of
ships—traffic control for those coming
and going through the Baltic Sea.

All atop an oval island (thirty meters
long, seventeen meters wide) built in 1937.
A fortress strong enough to withstand the
storms of the Øresund, a beacon of safety, a
guiding light in times of danger and treachery.

A FUTURE FORETOLD

The nautical life
filled Henny's days
from dawn to dusk.
The last thing she saw
every night
before she turned out the light
was a picture of the sea
her father had painted.
He had a little studio
in their attic and spent
almost all his free time
painting beautiful old frigates
and Danish sea battles.
Henny said,

*You could get seasickness from looking at
our walls. Once, Dad had painted a very
special painting, it was of a man who
had rowed to a buoy, like the Lighthouse
Authorities used to do regularly back
then. . . . I loved that painting and Dad
gave it to me for my . . . birthday and I
hung it over my bed.*

It shows a man in blue,

a member of the lighthouse crew,
precariously balancing
on a red-and-white buoy
wobbling in the waves
halfway between Denmark
and Sweden.
He's there, taking care
that the light on top
will shine bright,
a guiding light
for those who travel through the dark.

Two friends wait
in a rowboat nearby,
taking care,
ready to rescue him
should he fall.
The winds seem light,
the waves ripple softly for now,
but far off, clouds are gathering
on the horizon.
Take care.
Get ready.
Small light, shine bright.
A storm,
unlike any they had ever seen,
was coming. . . .

PART VI

Broadsided!

ATTACK!

The German invasion of Denmark
happened before breakfast.
Without warning,
at 4:15 a.m. on April 9, 1940,
Hitler's Nazis attacked Denmark
by land, sea, and air—
fifteen different locations at once—
in the shortest military operation
in history.

Henny, her family,
friends, and neighbors,
still in their nightgowns and pajamas,
awoke to a cacophony of sound—
all-alert sirens and
thundering German bombers
that blackened the skies overhead.

Henny's family said,

> *The Danes were clearly surprised, angry at*
> *their own military and politicians who had*
> *left the country defenseless, AND angry at*
> *the Germans.*

Most Danes were shocked and confused.
Rightly so!

The Germans had *vowed*
not to attack Denmark
under any circumstances
in a formally signed pact
just a year earlier!
Danes had thought
they could remain neutral.
They thought they were safe
from the Führer's fury,
but he had betrayed them
and their trust in peace.

Henny was just eighteen years old,
stumbling out of bed,
rubbing the sleep from her eyes,
when she found
that her homeland had been stolen.

HOW IT HAPPENED

In the dead of night,
a merchant ship
that usually carried a cargo of coal
slipped into Copenhagen
and docked near the
Danish army's headquarters
and King Christian X's castle.
Like a wolf in sheep's clothing
or a Trojan horse,
the ship disguised its true intent.
Inside there was no coal,
but German soldiers!
Secret hatches opened
and out poured the enemy!

Meanwhile,
German tanks
rolled across the roads,
German planes
roared across the skies.

All spewed Nazis
into Henny's homeland,
like red-hot magma

gushing from a volcano,
blackening the ground.
Though some astonished Danes
fought back at the castle
and the border,
the "battle"
lasted less than two hours.
The odds were hopelessly against them.
What could a tiny country
with 14,000 soldiers
(8,000 of them new recruits)
hope to accomplish
against the potential power of
the German Wehrmacht—
an army 2.5 million strong?

RUDE AWAKENING

As the sun climbed,
all of Denmark
stumbled out of bed
to find German aircraft
circling their cities and towns,
flying low,
just about three hundred meters
aboveground,
like dark raptors searching for prey.

A young boy
named Leo Goldberger
told of things falling from the sky.

From my window, I reached out to catch
[leaflets] coming down from the sky like
confetti. In . . . broken Danish the leaflet
appealed to all Danes to stay calm. The
German Wehrmacht had no aggressive
intentions, they only wanted to protect us
from the evil designs of the Allies. We were
urged to go about our daily business
as usual—as if nothing had happened.

A medical student
living with his sister reported,

> *I was awakened by the noise of aircraft*
> *flying low over Copenhagen. . . . We got*
> *dressed and hurried down to the streets,*
> *where we were stopped by German soldiers.*
> *Our suspicion was confirmed. Denmark*
> *was no longer a free country.*

Shocked and bewildered,
furious and ashamed,
the Danes watched
armed soldiers in green helmets,
brown-green uniforms,
and coal-dust-covered boots
march through the streets
and quickly take control
of the Danish towns,
setting up German signs
and stringing German
telephone lines.

Tiny Denmark—
about one-third the size of
New York State—

was overrun,
swarming with Nazis
like a blossom
beset by bees.

Outnumbered and outgunned,
the Danish people had to admit
there was little point in fighting.
Their land was flat;
there was nowhere to hide.
The German invasion,
code-named Operation Weserübung,
was a stunning success.
                For now.

WHAT DID HITLER WANT?

That's what Henny
wanted to know.
It was the question
on everyone's lips.

Germany's ravenous dictator
hungered for three things:

Denmark's railroad lines,
  farmlands,
      coastline.

Danish railroads could transport
iron ore to make German weapons.

Danish farms could serve up
pork, beef, and butter
for Germany's hungry people.

Danish coastlines could supply sites
for German naval stations
to battle Britain and the Allies.

What a bargain for Germany!
Pillaging and plundering,
Hitler gobbled up
what he wanted.
Danes like Henny,
her family,
and friends
paid the price.

AN UNEASY TRUCE

It was at six a.m.
that same morning,
that Denmark surrendered
under protest
and Henny's homeland
became a Nazi-occupied nation.

King Christian X
wrote in his personal diary,

> *I considered continued fighting*
> *pointless . . . and ordered shooting to be*
> *halted and negotiations to be initiated.*

He and the Danish parliament
agreed to cooperate with the enemy
IF
the people's rights,
including the long-held Danish right
to freedom of religion,
were kept intact.

Hitler agreed.

After all,
a peaceful occupation
meant only 20,000 Nazi men
were needed in Denmark
as opposed to
the 300,000 to 450,000 troops
needed to police Norway—
a country invaded on the same day,
which continued to fight back.

In Denmark,
King Christian
knew a fight would
only result in needless deaths.
So he issued a proclamation
to his beloved people.
Henny, her family, and fellow Danes
listened to his advice to stay calm,
to go about their business,
to behave as usual,
lest their actions provoke further harm.
    An uneasy truce had begun.

PART VII

On Watch

BALANCI

The
Danes'
king,
democratic
government,
police, army, and
navy were allowed to
stay in power to handle
the country's day-to-day issues.

The scales of justice tipped and teetered.

N G

A C T

The
Nazi soldiers
quickly seized
Denmark's
agriculture and
industry and built
seaside walls and forts
against Britain and Norway.

The future of Denmark hung in the balance.

THE KING'S BODYGUARDS

Doing late-morning errands
around town,
Henny had a good chance
of seeing the king.
King Christian X had not
gone into exile as
many other kings
and queens had
when Nazis occupied
their countries.
Denmark's king
proudly remained
in his castle
in his capital city,
a symbol for his people
of Danish patriotism.

Henny was delighted
that her king
still defiantly rode his horse
through the streets at eleven a.m.
every day as usual,
accompanied only by
two plainclothes policemen

on bicycles.
He would nod or shake hands
with his fellow Danes,
but never respond to salutes
from the Nazi soldiers.

One story tells of a German
asking about the relative lack
of bodyguards for the king.
A boy responded,
"We are *all* his bodyguards."
True or not, the oft-told story
reflects the fondness Danes felt
for their king.

In fact, many Danes wore
a small pin on their lapels
sporting the king's emblem.
It showed a crown with an insignia,
a *C* and an *X* inside,
for Christian X.
It was a small outward sign of
patriotism and protest.

WARTIME CONDITIONS

Henny, Bente,
and their father
still went to work
every day.
Carsten still went to school.
The *Gerda III* crew
still set out to sea.
Churches, businesses,
restaurants, theaters,
and museums
remained open.
Still,
        things weren't the same.

Blackout curtains blocked the light.
Air-raid sirens shattered nerves.
Clothing was rationed.
Everything was patched and recycled.
Leather shoes were scarce,
so wooden clogs caught on.
Boy scouts learned to darn socks.

Silk and later nylon stockings . . . could be
exchanged for just about anything during
the war if one could find them. Some

*Danish women would paint a seam up the
back of their tanned legs with makeup to
appear to be wearing silk stockings.*

Formerly plentiful food and gasoline
were rationed, too.

*Heating fuel became so scarce, many people
chopped up furniture or burned peat dug
up from bogs.*

Goods that had been exported to Britain
were redirected to Germany.
Imported food such as coffee, tea,
chocolate, and tropical fruits
like bananas disappeared.
But there was plenty of fish,
so people did not starve.
Henny wasn't bothered
by the rationing. She said:

*I will survive. [I'll] always be able to get
something to eat. Rationing is not the big
issue. Resisting the Germans . . . getting
our values right [is] the real focus.*

Life wasn't the same.
Still, the people coped.
Most listened to their king,
and few had plans
to fight back.
Patience was key.
This, too, would pass.

HITLER'S CANARY

Spring turned to summer,
summer to fall.
Life went on.
As one boy noted,
there were just
a lot of

> *armed guests—*
> *soldiers, airmen,*
> *naval and SS personnel,*
> *not to mention tanks—*
> *all over the place.*

When walking around town,
Henny, like every other adult,

was required to carry
an ID card called an Ausweiss
that could be demanded by a German
at any time. Without it,
one might be arrested on the spot
and held by the Nazis.

Hitler was pleased
and called Denmark
"a model protectorate."
He held it up as a shining example
of what Europe could look like
under the Third Reich's rule.
German Foreign Minister
Joachim von Ribbentrop
called Denmark "our flagship."
One Dane called it
"a state of paralysis."

Britain's prime minister,
Winston Churchill,
took another view.
He called Denmark
"the sadistic murderer's canary"
　　　—Hitler's pretty, powerless pet,
　　　　singing for its supper.

TAKING ORDERS

Henny's father
sometimes received orders
from the occupying officers.
> Move the buoys!
> Confuse the ships!
> Thwart an Allied invasion!

Change the shipping lanes?
Mask the coast's
shoals and rocks?
It was a foolish and
dangerous directive
endangering Danish vessels
and all nations
navigating their waters.

It was an insult to
Paul Sinding's expertise
and to his years of devotion
to safety at sea.

He refused.
The German
curtly informed Paul
that it was an order.

Paul replied,

> *I [receive] my orders from my own ministry*
> *and not from the German authorities.*

Later, he said.

> *I would not take part . . . without a direct*
> *order from the Department of the Navy,*
> *and then only under protest. This was*
> *considered a great insult by the Germans,*
> *however, nothing else was done by them.*

When the Danes stood up,
the Nazis often backed down.
Better not escalate tensions,
they thought.
It might risk
their relatively cushy jobs
in a cooperating country.
Better not to poke the hornet's nest.
The result was
a resentful stalemate.

As the months went on,
Paul Sinding's sense of justice
ignited a fighting spirit

beneath his dignified demeanor.
That spirit was deep
within his daughter as well.

THE COLD SHOULDER

Many Danes gave the Nazis
"den kolde skulder"—
the cold shoulder—
deserting shops and bakeries,
or moving out
to streetcar platforms
when Nazis would enter.

According to her family,
Henny would act with a
"sophisticated form of
civil disobedience."
She'd cross the street
if Nazi soldiers
were coming toward her.
She'd move to another seat
in a tram

if they sat next to her.
She'd move to another table
or turn her back
to them in a restaurant—
take on an air of "I do not see you."
While some might engage
the German soldiers
in civil conversation,
"they would not be met
with any encouraging smile
from her."

THE JEWISH QUESTION

One question worried the Danes:
How would Hitler treat
Denmark's Jewish citizens?

The Führer had made no secret
of his hatred
for the Jewish community,
defining them as an "inferior race."
He called them "vermin,"

"a race tuberculosis,"
and openly stated:

> *the ultimate goal must definitely be the
> removal of Jews altogether.*

The only question for Hitler
was how.
His first steps were to identify
and isolate them.

Hitler had labeled
German Jews years before
with the Nuremberg Laws.
Anyone with three or four
Jewish grandparents
was identified as Jewish,
whether they practiced Judaism
or not.
They were given identity cards
stamped with a red *J.*
Those with "non-Jewish names"
were given new middle names:
Israel for males,
Sara for females.

Anyone so labeled
had been stripped of
their rights and citizenship.
They were forbidden to marry Christians,
fired from legal and government jobs,
thrown out of schools and universities,
and forced to close their businesses.

Books that fostered
an "un-German spirit"
were burned by the Nazis,
many of them written by
Jewish intellectuals and scientists.

Yet after the Nazis invaded,
the Danish Jews
continued to live peacefully,
going to school,
work, and synagogue,
supported in every way
by their fellow Danes.

Danish authorities cautioned
their Jewish population
to avoid contact
with the Germans.

Jewish schools
and synagogues
were hooked up
to the Danish
police alarm system.

*They tried to live as normally as possible
but were constantly on the alert.*

How long
would Danish Jews be safe?
For Danes,
        that was the question.

JUST ANOTHER DANE

Denmark wasn't
completely free of anti-Semitism.
There was a small group
of Danish Nazis living there.
Politicians turned away
German Jewish refugees
in 1938,
fearing high unemployment,

just as many countries
turn refugees away
from their borders today.

But by the time
of the German invasion,
most of the more than
eight thousand Jews
living in Denmark
were fully accepted,
firmly established,
and thriving
in their country;
some, who called themselves
Viking Jews, had lived there
for centuries.

Hitler wasn't the first
to segregate Jewish people.
Venice built the first ghetto
to isolate Jews in 1516.
After that, rulers of
Poland, Russia, Germany,
and other
eastern European nations
followed suit.
Denmark never did.

Danes proclaimed
full equality for Jews
in 1814.

One man, Allan Hannover,
remembered:

> *As a boy I never had the feeling that I was*
> *different . . . my classmates never gave my*
> *Jewish background a second thought.*

Henny had Jewish girlfriends
and classmates
back at the Zahle's School,
and she thought of each one as
"just another Danish girl."

In Denmark, Hitler learned
that a Jew was treated as
just another Dane.
And he still needed
Denmark's food and supplies.
So he let them be.
       For now.

BLUE SKIES FOR BLUE EYES?

Why was Hitler
so easygoing with the Danes?
Many looked like Henny,
with fair hair and blue eyes—
an image that aligned
with Hitler's idea
of an ideal master race.
Was it their Nordic blood
that made Hitler so lenient
with Denmark's people?

Or was it that the king and the Danes
wouldn't tolerate his anti-Jewish laws
as other countries had?
      The Danes' support
      for their populace
      was soon to be tested.

PROFITS TO BE HAD

Not everyone minded
the occupation.
For some, there was
money to be made
from the occupying soldiers—
they were new customers
for Danish pastries and cream puffs,
pork, potatoes, herring,
rye bread, butter, and cream.
Merchants profited from selling
food and clothing;
manufacturers made money
helping to make weapons, radios,
airplane parts, and other pieces
of the German war machine.

So for some adults,
you went along to get along.
   Danish kids felt differently.

SMALL ACTS OF DEFIANCE

Danish children fought back
right from the start.
Only hours
after the German invasion,
a teenager named Arne Sejr
and his friends
were handing out leaflets
with their version
of the ten Commandments:

1. *You must not go to work in Germany or Norway.*
2. *You must work badly for the Germans.*
3. *You must work slowly for the Germans.*
4. *You must spoil their production machines and tools.*
5. *You must spoil whatever helps the Germans.*
6. *You must delay all German transports.*
7. *You must boycott all Italian [German ally] films and papers.*
8. *You must not buy or trade with the Nazis.*
9. *You must treat all traitors as they deserve to be treated.*
10. *You must defend every person persecuted by the Germans.*

**JOIN THE FIGHT FOR
DENMARK'S FREEDOM!**

Children might sport a
red, white, and blue beanie cap—
its design meant to mimic
the insignia of
the British Royal Air Force,
Germany's enemy in the sky.

Or kids might pinch
a German soldier
in a crowded street
and run for their lives.
Or pour sugar in the gas tank
of a German car.

But children like eighth grader
Knud Pedersen were warned
to be careful.

The occupation was on everyone's mind,
but . . . our teachers kept telling us not to
talk about it. Don't object. Don't mouth off.
We mustn't arouse the giant.

Fifteen-year-old Herbert Pundik
had been handing out
anti-Nazi newspapers.

He was scolded by
the chief rabbi
of Copenhagen, who said,

> *If you continue your illegal activities,*
> *you may jeopardize the entire Jewish*
> *community.*

Despite adult warnings,
these small acts of defiance
took root and would soon bloom
into the underground
Resistance movement,
with many teenagers
like Henny leading the way.

PART VIII

Stormy Seas

KNOCKDOWN

Hitler continued to tear
through Europe,
toppling cities and countries,
a wrecking ball
smashing centuries of civilization
in his quest for world rule.

After Poland
and Czechoslovakia
fell in 1939—
Boom!—
down went Denmark,
Norway, Belgium,
the Netherlands, Luxembourg,
and France in 1940.
Bam!
Yugoslavia and Greece
crumpled in 1941.
Crash!

Germany smothered news
of the knockdowns
when it began indirect control
of the Danish free press

three months after the invasion.
So in the days before television,
the internet, cell phones,
and twenty-four-hour news,
some Danes barely comprehended
the scope of Europe's destruction.

Crushing countries,
pulverizing peoples,
steamrolling societies,
Hitler paved the way for his own empire,
the towering Third Reich.

CHOOSING SIDES

As the fighting continued,
World War II became
a fierce face-off
between two superpowers.
In one corner,
the Axis powers—
Germany and its supporters,
Italy and Japan.

In the other, the Allies—
Great Britain, France, the Soviet Union,
and later, the United States and China.

Hitler kept pressuring Denmark
to choose sides.
At first, the Danes refused
to be drawn into the fight,
reminding Germans
of the conditions of surrender.

But Denmark was
an occupied country.
The scales of injustice
started to tip in Germany's favor.

To survive,
Denmark was forced
to give in to Germany
again and again.
They were forced
to sign papers and pacts
they did not want to sign,
boosting German propaganda.
One man commented,

*The German invasion left the Danish
people in a paralyzing state of despair,
frustration, anger, and shame.*

Listening to the news,
Henny was livid.
Were they giving in?
Why wouldn't her country
stand up to this bully?

Students marched in protest
and were beaten by police,
changing many from pacifists
to activists.

For Henny and other young people,
anger was the spark
that lit the fire.
They were of one mind
and Henny voiced their rage.

You dirty Germans, get out of my country!

LINES IN THE SAND

As Hitler continued
to pressure the Danes,
even he knew
to tread lightly on
three issues—
three deal breakers.

Denmark made it crystal clear
that the Danes would not agree to:
      1. the death penalty
      2. joining the German side of the war
      3. laws that discriminated
      based on race or religion.

These were three lines in the sand.
Nazis knew crossing them
would squash Danish cooperation,
which was feeding and fueling
the German war effort.
No, they wouldn't cross those lines.

      Yet.

FANNING THE FLAMES

There was a key difference
between the Germans and the Danes.
Germans believed in the State.
People must do
as they are ordered to do
by their leader.
Danes believed in the Individual—
in personal responsibility,
in human rights.

Danes often declared,

> *A man is a man even*
> *if he is not bigger than a mouse.*

That faith in the basic rights
of every living person
would fuel the fight
when, like David facing Goliath,
this tiny country would
take on the German giant.

PUSH AND PULL

For months,
Germany and Denmark
continued this dangerous game
of tug-of-war.
Germany would try to pull Denmark
to the dark side—
the side of the Axis powers.
Denmark would pull back,
determined to stay
out of the conflict,
to keep some semblance
of independence.

Hitler kept trying
to call the shots.
When he invaded
the Soviet Union in 1941,
he labeled Communists everywhere
The Enemy.
Those who believed in Communism,
even in Denmark,
must be arrested and imprisoned.

For Henny,
a girl raised by her father's
strong moral compass,
this was shocking.
Unjust.
Illegal.
The Communists
had committed no crime,
according to Danish law.
This was a violation of the
Danish constitution,
a clear threat
to Danish democracy.

But to keep the peace,
the Danish government
felt they had to obey.
The Danish police rounded up
known Danish Communists
(including three members
of the Danish parliament)
and sent them to prison.

Hitler pulled on
the tug-of-war rope
again and again.

Henny, her family,
and their fellow Danes
were stunned,
dismayed,
angry.

Politicians resigned.
Students marched again in protest,
furious with their government
for giving in to the German bullies.

They claimed they would rather
live under "Norwegian conditions"—
actively fighting Nazi rule
like their neighbor to the north—
than appear to be voluntarily
siding with the enemy.

Henny and her friends
couldn't have known that
the king and the government
were working frantically
behind the scenes to buy time.
Pretending to cooperate
with the Germans
would keep the peace

and protect their Danish Jews.
But time was running out.
Evil plans were already in the works.

A FINAL SOLUTION

Earlier that summer,
on July 31, 1941,
Nazis had issued wicked plans
in Europe.
Hitler's top deputy,
Hermann Göring,
commissioned a
"final solution."
The Nazis' initial ideas of
evacuating Jews to
another place
weren't working.
So now their thoughts
turned to extermination,
        to murder.

Mobile killing units
called Einsatzgruppen
had already rolled out,
and the mass murder
of Jewish people—
parents, grandparents, and children—
had begun.

YELLOW STARS

That fall,
Hitler decreed that all Jews
six years old and older
in the Great German Reich
must wear a large
yellow Star of David,
a badge sewn onto the clothes
on their arm or back or chest.
All were forbidden
in public
without a Jewish star,
labeled with their word for "Jew"—
"Jude" in Germany;

"Juif" in France;
"Jood" in the Netherlands.
Anyone who disobeyed
was fined
or worse.
>They could be imprisoned,
>>beaten, or even killed.

Hitler's mission to get rid of the Jews
was proceeding according to plan.
First: identify, separate, and label them.
Make them feel marked, humiliated, different.
Yellow stars would do just that.

A POPULAR MYTH

The king of Denmark
heard of the yellow stars,
discussed them with
his Danish prime minister
Vilhelm Buhl
and noted their conversation
in his diary.

He wrote that

> *If the request was made, the right attitude*
> *would be for all of us to wear the star of*
> *David.*

That conversation
was repeated by Buhl,
picked up and embellished
by a Norwegian cartoonist
and an American author.
From there, a popular myth arose
that the king was often seen
on his daily horseback ride around town
wearing the yellow Star of David.

The story grew!
Soon it was said that
all the people of Denmark
sported the star on their arms.
            These things never happened.

Unlike Jews elsewhere in Europe,
Jews in Denmark
were never forced
to wear the yellow stars.

But the story spread
because it reflected true feelings.

When Germany called upon Denmark
to solve "the Jewish question,"
Denmark's foreign minister replied,

> *There [is] no Jewish question in Denmark.*

The Danish government agreed.

> *As long as a Danish government*
> *has anything to say in this country,*
> *the Jews have no grounds for fear.*

The citizens of Denmark
were of one mind:
a threat to Danish Jews
was a threat to them all.
Any attempt to persecute the Jews
would trigger a nationwide revolt.

PART IX

Mutiny

UNJUST, UNFAIR

Everything was all wrong,
even in Henny's house.
One day she came home
to find that
her beloved painting—
the one her father
had painted and
given to her for her birthday—
was gone!

*I was very upset and went straight to
my father. I knew his craziness to sell
or give away his paintings. If someone
complimented him on a painting, he was
so flattered that he gave it to them.*

*Dad confessed that he had given my
painting to [a Jewish friend] . . . who
owned a small wine and tobacco store
in Christianshavn, where Dad shopped
daily. [His friend] had been to the studio
one day and seen the painting before it
was done, and apparently, he had coaxed
it out of him, probably a tobacco deal, and*

in the process Dad probably forgot to tell
him that the painting already was mine. I
was furious, cried, and made a scene, but
nothing helped. The painting was gone.

Henny was angry
at the merchant,
at her father,
at the world.
It was unjust, unfair.

Just like this war.

BUBBLE, BUBBLE, BOILING TROUBLE

Tempers flared.
Small bubbles
of rage, resentment, resistance,
started to simmer
among the Danish people.
Henny heard of
small unrelated groups—
doctors here,

students there,
underground journalists,
British radio broadcasters,
even young boys on bikes—
turning up the heat.
Henny's temperature
was rising;
the cauldron was brewing,
coming to a boil.
The bubble of
"cooperation"
was about to burst.

CALL A DOCTOR

Many doctors
were among the first
to join the Resistance.
In fact, British pilots
had special instructions
if they were shot down
over Denmark:
go to the nearest doctor—
a physician could prescribe help.

A medical student
turned Resistance leader explained,

> *Apart from your need for medical help . . .*
> *he will not give you away. . . . That's*
> *against his code. But there is also a great*
> *chance that he might be an active member*
> *of the Resistance movement.*

A physician would know people—
who to avoid, who would be helpful.
The doctor would have an automobile
so he could provide transportation.

> *Only physicians, ambulances, and other*
> *emergency vehicles were allowed to use*
> *gasoline and most gasoline stations were*
> *closed altogether.*

An estimated 427 physicians
and 177 medical students
joined the cause
in Denmark,
obeying the Hippocratic Oath.
They promised
to try to heal the sick,
to "refrain from doing

any injury or wrong"
and to keep whatever
they see or hear
"sacred and secret."

SPREADING SECRETS

Student unrest
grew all that year.
Small underground newspapers
such as *De Frie Danske*
and *Frit Danmark* flourished,
picking up news
radioed by the BBC.
Those early years produced
about 31 illegal papers;
five years later there were
530 with a circulation of
ten million copies!

These newspapers
were printed in secret,
by students

and Resistance fighters,
in basements and attics,
even in a dentist's office.
One was printed in the basement
of the Nazi headquarters!
They were dropped in mail slots
or left on windowsills.

When Henny picked one up,
she would have to be careful
to hide it,
read it in secret,
and take care
in discussing its news
in conversation.
An informant
could turn her in to the Nazis
and also endanger the paper's
writers and editors.

These newssheets
were verboten,
because they spread the word
about what was happening
in Denmark,
in Norway,

in Europe—
news the Nazis didn't want
the people to hear.
Reading them could cost you
your life.

RADIO NEWS AND VIEWS

It was the brainchild
of the BBC in England
to push a popular protest
in Denmark
called the *V* campaign.
Over the radio it broadcast:

> *We have the* V,
> *the good old Danish* V,
> *which stands for the Will to Win,*
> *for the Way to Victory—*
> *for the warnings of the enemy's final collapse,*
> *for the old Viking spirit,*
> *the* V *that means* We Will Win.

Suddenly, the *V* appeared
everywhere in Denmark.

Radio broadcasts, newspaper headlines,
and store advertisements used as many Vs
as they could.

GRAFFITI PROTESTS

Write *V*
the Danish *V.*
It stands for Victory
for Viking spirit, valiantly.
Write *V*!

ANOTHER V

Beethoven's Fifth Symphony
was frequently played on the radio,
the *da-da-da-DUM* of its opening notes
echoing the *dot-dot-dot-DASH*
of Morse code for the letter *V.*

After work, Henny and her family
would gather around the radio
as the BBC opened its show
with those first four notes
announcing "This is London calling."
Danish families
would listen in, hearing
the latest news of the war effort
from the Allied point of view.
Even children would listen,
including middle schooler
Knud Pedersen.

FIVE BOYS FIGHT BACK

Knud and his older brother, Jens,
had had enough.

> *Jens and I and our closest friends were
> totally ashamed of our government.*

Sons of a pastor,
the brothers recruited a cousin

and two friends
to form a club
to fight the Nazis.
They called it the RAF club,
after their heroes,
the Royal Air Force of Britain.
Their motto?
If the adults won't do something,
we will!
Their mission?
To fight back
until Churchill and the British
would free their country.

What could young boys do?
They could get in the way,
cause trouble,
create confusion.

They noticed that the Germans
had installed new signs in town
with black arrows pointing the direction
to Nazi barracks or headquarters.

Two of us backed up our bikes, counted off,
and pedaled full speed at the sign, one on

either side, and smashed the thing to the
ground. Then we twisted other signs around
so they pointed in the opposite direction.

What else could they do?
Use garden shears
to cut German telephone lines.

Their hours of operation?
Broad daylight.
Their getaway?
Their bikes.
(In fact, bikes would
become so important
to the Resistance,
Hitler would ban
all new bikes in 1944!)

It wasn't long before Knud
and the other middle schoolers
were wanted by the Nazis.
They had a price on their heads—
three hundred Danish kroner
(three months' wages)
for information leading to their arrest.

Ultimately,
some of the boys were captured
and sent to a German-run jail
for political prisoners
in Copenhagen.

The brothers Knud and Jens
evaded capture
and started an even bigger club—
the Churchill Club.
It pulled off twenty-five acts of sabotage
in broad daylight.

As far as propaganda was concerned,
they were of [the] greatest importance.

Like most Danes,
Henny heard of these boys,
saw the blue club symbol
they painted
on Nazi homes and cars,
and was inspired
by their kids' efforts to fight back.
If they could do it,
so could she!

ALARMING NEWS

At work, Henny's conversations
with the *Gerda III* crew
often turned to
the occupation and the war.

They discussed shocking news
of the mass extermination of Jews
in Western Europe.
The Nazis had denied it
in the Danish newspapers,
and the great majority
of the Danes
believed them.
Most people
couldn't bear to think
it might be true.
Or they thought,
it cannot happen here.

Some people, like
Henny's dear friend Isse
and her family, decided
to hunker down, to stay safe.
They would try as best they could

to live an ordinary life
during the occupation
and hope it would be over soon.
Henny's sister, Bente,
and brother, Carsten,
felt the same way.
Bente had her office work;
Carsten had school.
They wouldn't get involved.

HOLGER DANSKE

Those who had opposed
the occupation
from the beginning
began to join forces.
It angered them to see Danes
in friendly conversation
with the Germans.
Five men formed
a group called Holger Danske,
one of the largest
and most powerful

Resistance groups
of the war,
named for a legend.

THE LEGEND OF HOLGER DANSKE

The story was born in myth—
the tale of a knight
celebrated in poems of heroism
and in medieval songs
sung by minstrels and
troubadours.

As the story was passed down
through the ages,
Holger Danske
(a.k.a. Ogier the Dane)
took his place
in Danish folklore.

Denmark's famous author
Hans Christian Andersen

wrote a story about
the sleeping knight.

> *In Denmark there is an old castle named*
> *Kronborg. It lies on the coast of the*
> *Øresund, where hundreds of great ships*
> *pass through every day. But the most*
> *beautiful sight of all is old Kronborg, and*
> *in a deep, dark cellar beneath it, where no*
> *one ever goes, sleeps Holger Danske. He*
> *is clad in iron and steel and rests his head*
> *on his strange arms; his long beard hangs*
> *down over the marble table and has grown*
> *through it. He sleeps and dreams, and in*
> *his dreams he sees all that happens here in*
> *Denmark. . . . In his sleep he nodded and*
> *said, "Aye, remember me, you people of*
> *Denmark! Remember me! In your hour of*
> *darkest need I shall come!"*

For the Resistance fighters
calling themselves Holger Danske,
that hour had come.
The knight
would rise up to save his nation

and come to Denmark
in its hour of need.
              And so would Henny
                and two others
                    she would soon meet.

HENNY, MIX, AND JØRGEN

Three strangers—
Henny, a young woman,
Mix, a naval cadet,
and Jørgen, a medical student—
all in their twenties,
would soon rise up.
They would be drawn
into the same orbit,
fueled by
the same devotion to
social justice,
democracy,
and human rights.
They would soon bond as
friends,

allies,
and more.
Their three worlds
would converge
in a common mission,
a shared
fight,
flight,
plight.
Then their worlds
would diverge again,
their three separate trajectories
steered by
luck,
risk,
and betrayal.
Three paths that led
one to exile,
one to prison,
one to death.

PART X

Uncharted Waters

THE BIRTHDAY TELEGRAM CRISIS

September 26, 1942,
was King Christian's seventy-second birthday.
As always, it was celebrated
as a national holiday.
With school canceled,
kids crowded around
Amalienborg, the Royal Palace,
to watch the Red Guards parade
in full dress uniform
and to see the king
wave from the balcony.

Hitler sent the king a long, flowery
birthday greeting full of flattery.
He expected an elaborate, fawning
thank-you in return.
Instead the king sent a short
and unceremonious response.
"Meinen besten Dank. Chr. Rex"
("My utmost thanks. King Christian")

A joke circulating at the time
was that Hitler suggested
uniting the two countries

and the king . . . responded
he was too old to rule over
such a large country.

The Führer flew into a rage
at the king's curt thank-you note.
Hitler would show him!

PAYBACK

Hitler summoned
the German diplomat
overseeing the occupation
back to Berlin.
The Führer replaced
his white-glove approach
with an iron fist
by naming a top Nazi,
a Schutzstaffel (or SS) general,
to take charge.

This general had a reputation
as ambitious and merciless;

he was a mastermind
of the Gestapo
and the Einsatzgruppen—
the mobile killing units
that had massacred Jews in
the Soviet Union.
His nickname said it all—
"the Bloodhound of Paris."
After the war, a Danish medical
team examined him in prison
and called him "a psychopath."
His name was Werner Best.

The king did not receive Best
when he arrived in Denmark
with his grand title of
plenipotentiary
(meaning someone with full powers
to do as Hitler wished in Denmark).
Feigning illness, the king
sent his son instead.

Best, in time, would lead
to the worst of times.

THE IRON FIST

Harsher German leadership
squeezed the
Danish government.

As an officer in the navy,
Henny's father knew
that government employees
were not allowed
to rebel or strike.
The Danish Armed Forces
had pledged to maintain
a united front in line with
their parliament's policy
and their king's promise
of cooperation.
Henny's father
"made that point of view
known to his family,"
which only increased
Henny's frustration.
Why toe the line?
Couldn't adults
grasp what was going on?
What could she do

to knock some sense
into them?

For Henny,
the Nazis' iron fist
hammered home
the need to fight back.
But she remembered
her parents telling her,

> *Your family name is not an ordinary one.*
> *People will know who we are because your*
> *father is a naval commander.*

She couldn't compromise
her father's standing
in the navy.
He had made his wishes clear.
Given her fondness for her father,
she would respect that.
                For now.

FIGHTING BACK

For other young Danes,
Hitler's iron fist
was too heavy-handed.
Those who had only marched
in peaceful demonstrations
now stepped up to fight.

A young medical student
named Jørgen Kieler
was asked to take over
the illegal underground newssheet
Frit Danmark
after the original publishers
were arrested by the Nazis.
He readily agreed.
He recruited his sisters,
cousin, and fellow classmates
and his apartment became
their headquarters.
It wasn't easy.
They used manual typewriters
and Jørgen said,

> *None of us could touch-type, so we typed
> away with one finger.*

They printed and distributed
news of Allied wins
and German losses.
The papers encouraged Danes
to work at a slower pace,
make mistakes at work,
lose machinery parts,
misunderstand orders—
anything to slow the German
war machine.

But could they do more?
Should they consider sabotage?

TOUGH QUESTIONS

Jørgen and his family members
debated these issues.
He argued for action;
others pushed pacifism.

Jørgen asked one sister,

> *What will you do if the Gestapo enters*
> *. . . the room to shoot your younger brother?*

She answered,

> *Protect him with my body, but I will not*
> *carry arms.*

They debated:
How could they block
the Germans' grab for power?
How could they shorten the war
and end human suffering?

Was it ethical to use force?
Or was it imperative to fight evil?

These were tough,
"painful" questions,
decisions the family
didn't take lightly.
Jørgen said,

> *Taking part in sabotage meant taking*
> *personal risk, but also grappling*
> *with whether it was appropriate and*
> *responsible.*

There was only one thing
everyone could agree on:

the Nazis
and their "criminal war"
had to be stopped.

AIR RAIDS

Britain was doing its part
to thwart the Nazis,
sometimes with disastrous
results for the Danes.

In January 1943,
the Royal Air Force
dropped bombs on
Burmeister & Wain,
a work yard in the middle
of Copenhagen
building ships for the Nazis.
People were killed,
houses were leveled,
but the yard was not hit.

Jørgen realized that
on-the-ground sabotage
conducted by Danes
could better pinpoint
industries working for the Nazis
and protect Danish lives
at risk during air raids.

Jørgen struggled
with one issue:
How could he
ask others to risk their lives
while he only printed newspapers?

NEWS LIGHTS THE FUSE

Saboteurs were emboldened
by news of Allied wins.
In July 1943, Danes
targeted a new warship
the Nazis were building
in Odense to fight the Allies.
Boom!

They blew it up!
Violence, strikes,
and confrontations—
the work of Holger Danske
and other groups—
became more common,
building to several
occurring each day.
About 122 acts
of sabotage in 1942
grew to 969 a year later!
The news lit the fuse,
triggering more fighting.
Demonstrations
on the streets turned violent.
Patrols fired into the crowds.

EVERYDAY PERIL

Henny found it hard
to walk to work,
hard to dodge danger,
hard to mask her anger
at the Nazis.

The *Gerda III* crew
complained to Henny
about Germans taking over
Drogden Lighthouse.
Now the Nazis lived with
the lighthouse keepers
and monitored all
who came and went.
The *Gerda* crew had to watch
what they said and did
delivering their supplies.
German ears were listening.

In August 1943,
the Nazis
painted over
the lighthouse's bright
red and white stripes,
camouflaging it from the Allies.
They used its antiaircraft gun
to shoot at British planes.
The British fired back
and the lighthouse
was hit several times,
putting Henny's friends
in harm's way.

Just like Denmark,
Henny, the lighthouse keepers,
and the *Gerda III* crew
were caught in the middle,
as growing violence
threatened their everyday lives.

AUGUST UPRISING, 1943

Late that summer,
tensions came to a head
when Danish workers
went on strike in seventeen cities.

Infuriated,
Hitler summoned
his man Werner Best
back to Berlin.

The day Best left Denmark,
a boy on a bike
delivered a crate of beer
to the Copenhagen Forum,

a huge exhibition hall
converted and about to open
as barracks for German soldiers.
The boy dropped off the crate
        and ran!

Inside were not beer bottles,
but one hundred pounds
of explosives,
planted by Holger Danske.
The grand building
meant for German housing
shattered in shards
to the ground.

THE CRACKDOWN

The crackdown was swift.
On August 28, 1943,
Hitler sent Best back to Denmark
to deliver an ultimatum—
obey these new rules or else:
        No more strikes.

No public meetings of more than five people.
All must obey an 8:30 p.m. to 5:30 a.m.
curfew.

Imagine Henny hearing this news!
Now she was forbidden
to be seen with five friends.
She was twenty-two years old
and she would have to rush home
by 8:30 p.m.
But sometimes the curfew
worked in her favor.
Stranded at a party,
the Germans' rule gave her
a good excuse
to spend the night
at a friend's house.

We had a great time and we never knew
if we [would be] alive tomorrow, so better
taste the good life NOW!

But then the news grew worse.
The Nazis' new rules were backed
with lethal threats:
now acts of sabotage,

possession of firearms,
or attacks on German soldiers
would be punishable by death.

The Nazis demanded that
the Danish police
catch the saboteurs,
sentence them to death,
and carry out the executions.
Of their own people!

The Danes' answer
to the German ultimatum?
NO!
The Danish king
and government resigned.
The Nazis immediately
shut down telephone,
telegraph, and mail services.
They surrounded
the king's palace
and he was placed
under house arrest.
Many Danish soldiers
were arrested
and held against their will.

Nazis took control
of the Danish army
and took aim at the navy.
          The navy was ready for them.

ONE STEP AHEAD

Years before,
the Danish navy
had planted bombs
on their own ships.
They hid two-and-a-half-,
five-, and ten-kilo bombs,
each with a ten-minute timer,
in each commanding officer's safe.
Better to blow their own ships
sky high
than let the Nazis have them.
Now the moment
of the long-anticipated attack
          had arrived.

STORMING THE DOCKS

Boom! Boom! Boom!
Henny's family
and the people of
Copenhagen awoke
on August 29
to the sounds of bombs
and the smells of smoke,
detonating chaos and confusion
among the sleepy citizens.

Operation Safari
was under way!
Nazis had stormed
the naval dockyards at 4 a.m.

By 4:08 a.m.,
Danish vice admiral Vedel
had ordered the signal K N U
dispatched to all units,
authorizing the navy's plan
to sink the ships.
Danish ships at sea
received the coded radio message:
"Seek Swedish waters."

The Danes in the Royal Dockyard
in Copenhagen knew what to do:
they raised the bridges
that connected the islands,
causing detours and delays
for the Germans.
One sentry guarding a bridge
to the Holmen base
proved the power
of what one person can do.
He obeyed the navy's order
to open the bridge,
blocking the Nazis' advance,
and went one step further.
He conveniently "lost" the handle
that operated the bridge.

Throwing the handle into the water when
the Germans showed up was something he
did on his own initiative.

It stopped
about four hundred
German soldiers
long enough
for the Danes

to set off the bombs
to burn or scuttle
the fleet.

The first charge exploded at 4:13 a.m.
By 4:35 a.m., the deed was done.

In less than half an hour,
thirty-two Danish warships—
one coastal defense ship,
six torpedo boats,
six mine layers,
nine submarines,
one floating workshop,
one ocean patrol boat,
five minesweepers,
one survey ship,
and a couple others—
were sinking or on fire,
rather than letting the Germans have them.

At sea, two ships were safe in Greenland;
one old torpedo boat
and three small minesweepers
reached Sweden.

When Henny found out
what was happening,
she was "ecstatic."
Scuttling the ships meant Danes
were really fighting back now.
It was about time!
When the smoke cleared,
it was with a mix of
"big sorrow *and* pride"
that Henny's father, family,
and townspeople viewed
the destruction in their harbors.
It was an especially sad day
for Henny's father.
Ships were supposed to sail
and fight the enemy,
not sink to the bottom of the sea.

Ultimately, the Germans took charge,
recovering fourteen
of the fifty-two ships
in the Danish fleet unharmed,
eventually raising and repairing
the damaged vessels,
and confining Danes
involved in the destruction
to their barracks.

A German navy officer told Vedel
that the Danes had done
what the Germans would have done
in the same situation.

In all, Operation Safari resulted
in more than 4,600 Danes captured;
twenty-three to twenty-six were killed,
and forty to fifty were wounded.
But now the Nazis
needed to get German ships
to sweep for mines
laid by the Allies,
to keep the sea-lanes to Norway open,
and to conduct surveillance along the coast.
Fewer ships meant fewer resources
for the German war effort.

The Allies took note
of Denmark's courage.
"Hitler's canary"
was showing its claws.

MIX IN THE MIX

When the Danish warships
sped for Sweden,
one young naval cadet
named Erik Koch Michelsen,
nicknamed Mix,
wasn't aboard.
He was on leave in town.
In a desperate attempt to rejoin
his fellow shipmates,
Mix grabbed a small boat
from his parents' summerhouse,
painted the white hull blue
for camouflage,
rigged a sail,
and at ten p.m. that night,
set off to cross the Øresund
to Falsterbo, Sweden.

> *I expected to be over the next morning at*
> *6–7 o'clock. At first it went quite well. . . .*
> *At 4 [a.m.] the wind changed, and it began*
> *to blow . . . strongly . . . and pour down,*
> *and the visibility was very poor. . . . Then*
> *I rowed on against the current and wind.*

Shortly afterward the mast broke, . . . I
saw the sail drifting away. I continued to
row in the supposed right direction. . . .
I never wanted a compass so much as
then. . . . I became rather exhausted. . . .
The current was against [me] and quite
strong, about 3 knots.

Mix had "not fully recovered
from . . . polio"
that had impaired
one of his hands,
So it was slow going.
He lost his way in the gray
and nearly died.

At 7 [a.m.] I gave up . . . lay down . . .
and let myself drift. . . . It seemed to me
that time stood still. I was shivering with
cold, . . . I don't remember any more until
it was 9:30. . . . I was freezing, and the
[boat] was half full of water. . . . Far away
[I thought] I saw a big steamer. It was the
Drogden Lighthouse.

Like a beacon of things to come,
the Drogden Lighthouse
beckoned him ashore.
He didn't know it yet,
but in time,
that lighthouse
would lead him to Henny.

PULLED ASHORE

Landing at the lighthouse,
Mix didn't drown,
but he was far from safe.
Nazis living
with the lighthouse keepers
destroyed Mix's boat
and held him for eight days.

But Mix was surprised to find
that the soldiers were
somewhat friendly
and wanted to talk politics.

Curiously, [the Germans] were almost
all convinced that Germany would win
the war, but they listened willingly to my
views . . . They had a strange respect for all
Scandinavians, and they strongly insisted
that they and we were of the same race. . . .
I explained to them that . . . Scandinavian
countries . . . looked upon Germany as the
enemy and the ruffian of Europe.

Conversation over!
On September 6,
Mix was picked up
by a German motorboat
and taken back to Denmark
to join the navy men
being held in the Royal Dockyards.
Arriving at Holmen,
Mix saw the scuttled ships
and felt "very sad," but also

immensely proud . . . at the successful
destruction that had taken place.

Those eight days
at the lighthouse

had been fateful days for Mix.
He had gotten to know
the lighthouse keepers,
and made friends with
the crew of the lighthouse tender
Gerda III.
When the Nazis weren't looking,
the men whispered news of the war
and the Resistance
and what they could do to help.
Mix learned about
the Danish Lighthouse
and Buoy Service
and about the crew's boss,
Paul Sinding.
In a few short weeks,
Mix would learn
of Paul's daughter Henny too.
It was the start of something big!

PART XI

Gale Warnings

A NEW MAN IN CHARGE

Werner Best was out!
Hitler replaced him with his rival
Hermann von Hanneken,
the general of the infantry,
who promptly declared
a military state of emergency.

The country was no longer
a "model protectorate"
governed by their beloved king.
A Nazi military general
was in command
and the country was now
enemy territory
under martial law.

NEW LAWS OF THE LAND

Diplomacy was dead.
The Germans had squashed
the Danes' democracy

and Danish law and order.
The Danes saw that
their leaders were no longer
able to protect them.

"The Law" was now the Nazis' law
and the Danes knew that law was unjust.
The simmering Danish Resistance
boiled over.

Henny's father,
the upright royal navy commander
with his strong moral compass
and sense of what was right,
knew the German laws were wrong.
He knew the time had come
to fight back,
to do the right thing.

After August 29, 1943, the Lighthouse
Authorities got involved in illegal
work. . . . We acquired some illegal radio
transmitters, stole shiploads of cargo from
the German-occupied Naval Dockyard,
delivered explosives to the Resistance.

But of course,
the commander didn't speak
of this with his family.
Henny didn't know
that her father
and his colleagues
were now devising
"ideas of how best
to annoy the Germans."

MIX MEETS JØRGEN KIELER

Mix, the naval cadet
held at Drogden Lighthouse,
was now interned
at the navy base.
But there weren't
many Germans
to guard them
and passes were easy to fake.
Mix sneaked out of the base
with a fellow cadet named Svend
to visit Svend's cousin—

who happened to be
Jørgen Kieler.

Jørgen immediately saw that
Mix was a natural leader.
He had a "big smile,"
"lively eyes," and
a "keenness and impatience
to get going."
Mix was passionate to "restore
Denmark's self-respect"
and to safeguard "the good name
of the country and . . . the navy."
He was clever too.
He and Svend had smuggled
weapons out of the naval base
under the Nazis' noses.
They delivered them to Jørgen
to use for sabotage.
Mix quickly joined the group
working with Jørgen.
Jørgen said,

> *I had great confidence in [Mix] right from*
> *the start and knew we would soon become*
> *good friends.*

SAVING FACE

Meanwhile
the German leadership
in Denmark
was struggling.
Werner Best felt
disgraced in Hitler's eyes.
How was he
to regain the Führer's favor?
Best had an idea:
give Hitler what he wanted most—
      Denmark's Jews!

On September 8, 1943,
Best sent telegram #1032
to Hitler's minister of foreign affairs,
Joachim von Ribbentrop,
recommending a plan
to capture them.

Measures should now be taken toward a
solution of the problem of the Jews . . . as
long as the present state of emergency exists.

He warned
of further unrest

and strikes.
He told Hitler's advisers
he would need more police
to arrest and deport

> *some 6,000 Jews (including*
> *women and children)*
> *at one sweep.*

And he would need ships
to transport them to Germany.

THE TIP-OFF

Werner Best needed
someone in Denmark to help.
He chose Georg Duckwitz,
a German in charge of shipping.

On September 11, 1943,
he divulged the plan
to Duckwitz,
telling him of his telegram.
Duckwitz was horrified!

Although German,
he had spent many years
in Denmark,
had close friends there,
even called the country
"his chosen fatherland."
He had worked hard
to help develop
a peaceful occupation
and understood
that taking the Jews
would cause a revolt.

Duckwitz jumped on a plane
to Berlin to intercept
Best's message.

Too late!
The Führer had seen it,
          and approved it.

Delighted with this plan,
Hitler put Werner Best
in charge again
and sent extra Nazi police
to help him.

THE BREAK-IN

Before Nazis
could round up the Jews,
they had to identify them.
On September 17,
the Gestapo,
wearing civilian clothes,
broke into
Ny Kongensgade 6,
the Jewish Community Center
in Copenhagen.

The Gestapo ransacked
the library,
holding employees
at gunpoint.
What was stolen?
Genealogies,
marriage registries,
lodge meeting notes—
any records revealing
the names and addresses
of the city's Jews.
The Nazis added their stash
to the registers of Jewish births,
deaths, and marriages

they had seized
in similar raids.

They offered no excuse
for this crime.
They took them
because they could,
because they had guns,
because they were stronger.

The Danes knew now
that anything could happen.
The Gestapo had the names of the Jews.
Could a roundup be far behind?

FIRST WORD

A law student
in Jørgen Kieler's group
first heard word
of the roundup
on September 26.
Jørgen Jacobsen,

alias Tromle ("the drum"),
received a phone call
from a mysterious source
and tried to sound the alarm.
His own father and brothers
didn't believe him.
Jørgen Kieler said,

> *We knew we had to warn as many people*
> *as possible as soon as we could. We did not*
> *know many Jews, but like Tromle and*
> *many others, we found that our warnings*
> *were taken with a pinch of salt. The*
> *country had been occupied for three and a*
> *half years without anything happening.*
> *Why should anything happen now?*

STAY OR GO?

No one knew for sure
what might happen.
Some Jewish families
disappeared,

leaving home
for small rural farms
or hiding in the woods.
A few died by suicide.
Others sat tight,
trying to avoid attention.
They worried an exodus
would incur the Nazis' wrath
and punish those left behind.
Besides,
where could they go?
Uncertainty and tension
grew stronger
with each passing day.
What if the rumors were true?

RUMORS WHIRLING

Round and round rumors flew—whirling, twirling, wheeling, reeling. A spiraling galaxy of fear collapsed in on itself, with gravity pulling hope and light into a black hole of despair.

FURIOUS

Henny didn't know
anything for sure,
but she too heard
the rumors.
She "felt furious"
that the Nazis would

> interfere with our Danish people.
> [The Jews] were Danes like we were.
> We never divided [ourselves] up
> into Danes or Jews. The Danish Jews,
> they were just Danes.

Something had to be done,
but what?
Henny was at a loss.
How could she respect
her father's wishes
and still help?
Frustration mixed with fury
was a bitter brew.

SCRAMBLING

In the meantime,
politicians were panicking.
Even the king had heard
talk of a Jewish roundup
and sent Werner Best
a letter of protest,
warning that

> *special measures against a group of people*
> *who have enjoyed full civic rights in*
> *Denmark for more than one hundred years*
> *could have the most severe consequences.*

Best denied anything
was afoot.

Duckwitz knew better.
He flew to Sweden
to ask their neighbor
to take in Denmark's Jews.

No dice.
Sweden was neutral
and didn't want to anger Germany.

SPILLING SECRETS

Duckwitz continued
to quietly spread the word
of the coming raid.
He tipped off his friends.
He enlisted
the German harbor commander,
who disapproved of the roundup
and helped by
taking police boats
out of commission for repairs.

Duckwitz knew he couldn't stop
the coming disaster,
but he did all he could
to sound the alarm
without tipping off the Germans.
In his diary he wrote:

> *I will assume responsibility for everything*
> *I am going to do. . . . good deeds can never*
> *be wrong. There will be no detour from*
> *the road I have taken. There are, after all,*
> *higher laws. I will submit to them.*

THE DATE IS SET

On Tuesday, September 28,
Duckwitz was summoned to
Werner Best's office
and given the final word:
the arrest and deportation
of the Danish Jews
would occur three days later—
that Friday night,
October 1.
It would be the end
of the second day
of Rosh Hashanah,
the Jewish New Year,
and the Shabbat Shuvah.
Given the holidays
and the curfew,
Best knew Jews
would be at home.

SOUNDING THE ALARM

Three days!
Duckwitz knew
he had to do more
to get the word out
without alerting the authorities.
Who could he tell
to reach the most people?
He decided to tip off
a prominent Danish politician—
Hans Hedtoft.
He set up a meeting
and told him,

> *Now the disaster is about to occur. . . .*
> *Ships are going to anchor in the harbor*
> *of Copenhagen. Your poor Jewish fellow*
> *countrymen who will be found by the*
> *Gestapo will be forcibly transported to the*
> *ships and deported to an unknown fate.*

Hedtoft later told
of their mutual outrage.

> *[Duckwitz's] face was white with*
> *indignation and shame. . . . I became*

speechless with rage and anxiety. This
was too diabolic. [Duckwitz] personally
did everything that was possible to save as
many human lives as he could.

THE WARNING!

Hedtoft sprang into action.

> *I divided the job among some friends. . . .*
> *We went in all directions. I chose first*
> *to visit the chairman of the Jewish*
> *Community, C. B. Henriques. . . . He only*
> *said two words, "You lie." It took some*
> *effort to persuade him to believe me.*

Another man Hedtoft told
would alter the course
of World War II
    for the Danes,
      for the world.

Hedtoft revealed the news
to his friend Niels Bohr—

a Dane, a Jew,
and a Nobel Prize–winning scientist.
Bohr had led research
into a new science
at the University of Copenhagen—
the pursuit of nuclear energy.

It could be used for peace,
but both the Axis and Allies
knew it could also be used for war,
for building a weapon
unlike any the world had known—
the atomic bomb.

Germany was working
on such a bomb.
So were the British.
And the Americans.
The race was on;
whoever had Niels Bohr
would probably win the race.

The Nazis couldn't risk
this Jew's escape to the other side.

A WANTED MAN

But escape he did!
He was warned on September 29,
the day Rosh Hashanah
would begin at sundown.
Instead of beginning
their New Year's prayers
and celebrations that evening,
Bohr and his family hid
in a cottage
in Copenhagen.
They were picked up by a fisherman,
who took them to two rowboats.

> *Some distance out to sea the rowing boats*
> *[were] hailed by a larger fishing boat . . .*
> *all the refugees were taken on board, and*
> *they were driven toward the Swedish coast.*

They landed in Limhamn at 5 a.m.
and Bohr boarded a train
for Stockholm at 6:55 a.m.
The Gestapo chased after Bohr.
They couldn't allow him
to get to England

knowing all he knew.
It could change the course of the war.

Bohr was wanted,
                    dead or alive.

OFF TO SEE THE KING

Despite the danger to his life,
Bohr met with the king of Sweden
and implored him
to shelter his countrymen.
The king agreed
and the announcement
headlined news
around the world.
A wooden plane called
a Mosquito bomber whisked
Bohr off to England.

His escape
had far-reaching consequences.
Thanks to Bohr,

Sweden's king provided
safe harbor for Danish Jews;
without it, all rescue efforts
would have been in vain.
And Bohr's research
did indeed lead to
the atomic bomb,
which controversially
ended World War II
in Japan
two years later.

But for now, the war raged on.
And the roundup
of the Danish Jews
was just days away.

TELLING THE PEOPLE

As Bohr was escaping,
word of the impending disaster
reached Rabbi Marcus Melchior.
On the morning

of Wednesday, September 29,
the rabbi interrupted early services
at the Copenhagen synagogue
with a shocking statement.
He said,

> *We have no time now to continue prayers.*
> *We have news that this coming Friday*
> *night, . . . the Gestapo will come and*
> *arrest all Danish Jews. They have a list of*
> *addresses and they will come to the home of*
> *every Jew and take us all to two big ships*
> *waiting in Copenhagen harbor, and on to*
> *camps on the continent.*
>
> *There are two things you should do.*
> *Number one, you should stay away from*
> *your homes on Friday night. . . . Number*
> *two, pass this news on to as many friends,*
> *family, whomever you can, so that they also*
> *know to leave home by Friday.*

SUNDOWN

That very evening,
Wednesday, September 29,
was the start of Rosh Hashanah—
the Jewish New Year,
honored by Jews
as the birthday of the world.

That year, as every year,
Rosh Hashanah
was the start of
the High Holy Days,
a ten-day period
leading up to
Yom Kippur
(the Day of Atonement).
Beginning at sundown
each year,
it is a time
when Jewish families
rejoice,
look inward,
reflect on their lives,
make amends.

It was and is
always
a time of family,
home, and prayer.
A sacred time
of new beginnings.

It was a special wickedness
that made the Nazis
choose this holiday,
one of Judaism's
holiest times,
and a Friday night—
the Shabbat Shuvah—
as the night of the roundup.

MOBILIZING MAGIC

After the announcements
made by the rabbi and others,
word of imminent danger
raced across Copenhagen
(the home of more than
95 percent

of the Danish Jews)
and the countryside beyond.
More than thirty to forty thousand people,
including Henny, her family,
and the crew of *Gerda III*, mobilized
to help Jewish families disappear.

H FOR HELPING HANDS

Ambulance drivers
Boy Scouts
Cross-country runners
Dentists
Elementary school kids
Fishers
Grocers
Housekeepers
Industrialists
Janitors
Kitchen workers
Lighthouse keepers
Ministers
Neighbors
Officers

Physicians
Quartermasters
Radio operators
Shopkeepers
Taxi drivers
Underground Resistance fighters
Volunteers
Warehouse workers
X-ray technicians
Yacht captains
Zookeepers

Simple as that.
Danes would not allow
this roundup to happen.

HENNY TO THE RESCUE

It was on one of these
"last days in September"
as word of the roundup
flew around town
that Henny joined
the effort to aid the Danish Jews.

The *Gerda III* crew
asked if she could speak
with them down at the boat.
Henny said,

> *The crew was gathered and they looked*
> *very serious. And I said, "What's the*
> *matter?" They were always very full of*
> *good spirit, but that day they looked very*
> *solemn.*

The crew had heard word
of the roundup
through Jørgen Kieler's group.

> *They said they'd been thinking . . . that*
> Gerda III *was ideal to sail refugees to*
> *Sweden, but it was an official boat and*
> *they couldn't just steal it. . . . They asked*
> *me, could I fix that? . . . Could I try to talk*
> *to my father and ask if they could take the*
> *boat and use it for that purpose?*

It made a lot of sense:
Gerda III had permission
to sail all the way out
to the five-kilometer border

and it was going
to Drogden Lighthouse
every day anyway.
The crew was searching
for some sort of
unofficial permission
to use the boat for
unofficial duties.
Henny quickly realized
she could solve the problem.
She could ask her father,
the crew's boss.

A second problem was
moving *Gerda III*
from the naval yard
swarming
with Nazis.

If they were going
to help the Jews,
they needed a quieter dock
where it would be
easier to sneak
the refugees aboard.
Henny listened carefully.

Her mother's words
from her childhood
echoed in her head:

> If somebody comes asking you for help, and
> you are in a position to help, then you must
> help!

Henny agreed.
Here—*finally!*—
was a way
she could fight back.
She would do
whatever she could.

THE TALK WITH DAD

Henny didn't waste
any time
and strategically
chose the place
for the conversation
with her dad.

Henny went to her
father's office
right away.
She didn't want to ask
at home and risk her mother
hearing the conversation.
Henny knew her mom
would worry.

*I went straight into it and asked Dad not
to put out an APB [all points bulletin] on*
Gerda III, *and not to blame the crew if
sometimes, the boat wouldn't sail its usual
route on its usual schedule.*

I also asked Dad to provide a new berth for
Gerda III *in Christianshavn Canal across
from Wilders Plads, so it could be docked
there overnight.*

*Last, I asked Dad to advise the lighthouse
keeper at Drogden Lighthouse to look the
other way at the irregularities in* Gerda
III's *sailing. . . . I promised . . . the boat
would take care of its daily duties, and that
the work that the crew were hired to do
[would be] done.*

Henny never mentioned
the word "Jews,"
but her dad understood.

> *Of course, Dad was okay with it all. He
> didn't ask any questions. The less he knew
> the better, but obviously, he knew exactly
> what it all concerned, and he promised
> to do like I asked. Actually, I think he
> was very pleased that the Lighthouse
> Authorities were involved in helping with
> the refugee transportations.*

As she turned to go,
Henny could tell her dad
was nervous for her.

> *Dad just looked at me and said, "Be
> careful, whatever it is you are getting
> involved in, my girl."*

A NEW BERTH

It didn't take long
for the commander
to do as Henny asked.

> *Already the next day, my father had found*
> *a new place for* Gerda III *and then we*
> *started working.*

Now the boat was docked
across from Wilders Plads,
far from the Nazis
in the naval yard
and just a short walk
from Henny's house.
It was situated
beside Hans Just's warehouse
off Strandgade
(Strand Street).

> *The crew knew somebody who worked*
> *there. They had permission to borrow the*
> *attic.*

> *There was a door at [the side of the*
> *warehouse where] we could sneak in.*

It was the perfect place
to hide the Jewish refugees
until it was time for them to sail.
Henny and the crew of *Gerda III*
rushed around making preparations.
And they were not alone.

WARNING! WARNING!

Stories abound
of how other people
sounded the alarm.
Even to strangers.

There was no general awareness in
Denmark of who was or was not Jewish.
Many were surprised to discover that the
people next door were Jews.

One ambulance driver
named Jørgen Knudsen
pulled a telephone directory
from a phone booth,
noted Jewish-sounding names,

and drove to their addresses
to warn them.
If they had no place to go,
he whisked them in his ambulance
to Bispebjerg Hospital,
where Dr. Karl Køster would
hide them in hospital beds.

Nine-year-old Jette Borenhoff
was tipped off by the nuns at her
Catholic school.

Bookstore owner Mogens Staffeldt
biked around town
to alert friends and customers
of the coming disaster.

Fifteen-year-old Herbert Pundik
was sitting in French class
when he was called into the hall
and warned by his headmaster.
A classmate handed Herbert
a Boy Scout compass
as he rushed to get away.

I was home in ten minutes. There was no time to say goodbye to friends. . . . The worst was not the fear of [going] from a carefree schoolboy into a hunted Jew, . . . but seeing my parents so scared and out of control.

Herbert packed a few clothes,
but had to leave favorite things
like his stamp collection behind.

From one hour to the next, we had become homeless.

Nine-year-old
Kirsten Meyer Nielsen
remembered her classmates
envied her.
She got to go to Sweden
where they had chocolate and
chewing gum.

Grete Michel was sitting down to
a Rosh Hashanah dinner in the home
of her mother-in-law.
A neighbor knocked to warn them
of the anti-Jewish raid.

As they were hastily packing,
they received

> three completely spontaneous visits from
> people offering to put the family up, look
> after their home and property, and arrange
> transport out of the country.

Rabbi Melchior,
who had sounded the alarm,
needed a hiding place himself
along with his wife
and five children.
But first he called
a Lutheran minister in Ørslov,
ninety-seven kilometers southwest.
He asked him to hide
the holy objects of the synagogue—
the scrolls of the Torah,
the silver candelabra,
the prayer books.
The minister readily agreed;
he would hide the rabbi's family too.

Two days were all the Jews had,
two days of what should have been

a loving family holiday.
From Wednesday morning
to Friday evening,
Danes scrambled to make room
for friends, neighbors, and strangers.

A Danish proverb said it all:

> *If there is room in your heart*
> *there is room in your house.*

WHY DID THEY HELP?

> *It was exactly the same as having your*
> *neighbor's house on fire. Naturally you*
> *wanted to do something about it.*
> —RICHARD EGE, PROFESSOR, INSTITUTE OF
> BIOCHEMISTRY

> *It was my duty as a Dane, as a human*
> *being.*
> —MOGENS STAFFELDT, BOOKSHOP OWNER

I would have done it for anybody . . . in need of help. . . . For me, it was not a Jewish problem, it was a simple humanity problem.

—EBBA LUND, THE GIRL IN THE RED CAP

I felt it had to be done. I just couldn't stand by and do nothing while friends of mine were being persecuted. I would have helped anyone to escape from the Gestapo.

—JØRGEN KNUDSEN, AMBULANCE DRIVER

All decent people did. Because of sympathy with poor, persecuted people, who came to us confidently placing their lives and fates in our hands.

—GERDA BERTELSEN, LYNGBY RESCUE GROUP

The Germans' picking on Jews made as much sense to me as picking on redheads.

—DR. KARL KØSTER, SURGEON AT BISPEBJERG HOSPITAL

We were not heroes, but we were infuriated that the situation in Denmark in 1943 became so serious that our Jews should pay

for it, so everybody who got the chance did
whatever they could to help.
—HENNY SINDING

Danes everywhere
rushed to the rescue,
frantic to help.
Time ticked down.
　　And then, the unthinkable happened.

PART XII

Mayday

DARKNESS

The terrible day arrived.
October 1.
Shabbat Shuvah began
just before sunset.
The Nazis expected Jews
to be home, at prayer,
reading the Torah,
reflecting on repentance.
And yet no Danish trespass
could match the Nazi crime
about to occur.

Darkness seeped into the streets.
Two ships and a train
with forty cattle cars
stood in the shadows,
at the ready
to transport the Jews
as soon as they were captured.

Two hours before midnight
the Gestapo
shut down the phone lines.

They blocked the roads
and German policemen
fanned out in fifty flatbed trucks
to begin their deadly sweep
of Jewish homes.

Banging on doors,
the Nazis found a surprise
in store.

Almost no one was at home.

CLOSED DOORS

German police
were under orders
to knock *on* doors,
not to knock down doors.
They were to take people,
not property.
If no one answered,
police were to leave
in peace.

One Jewish couple
was sound asleep
and escaped arrest
because they did not hear
that ominous knock.

Why the policy of politeness?
The Germans reasoned
that breaking and entering,
destroying property,
and theft were crimes.
They couldn't have Danes
think that they were uncivilized,
that they were criminals.
Could they?

IN HIDING

How did the families disappear?
Part of the Bogratschew family
hid just next door
with a neighbor in
their apartment building.

The mother heard Nazis
pounding on their door
but when no one answered,
they did not break down the door.
To her great relief, they just left.

Miriam Ruben, age five,
told of sleeping
with her mother and father
in a stable.

Harry La Fontaine
disguised a rabbi
by dressing him
in women's clothing.

Fifteen-year-old Niels Bamberger
and his family were hidden
by their grocer.
The grocer called friends in the
Resistance movement,
saying, "I have six tons of potatoes.
Can you come and pick them up?"
"Potatoes" was code for *people*,
used in case the Nazis were tapping
the phones.

Doctors admitted healthy Jews
to the hospital
and hid them in hospital beds
under fake names
like Hansen, Jensen, or Petersen.
They even gave them
phony medical charts
listing fake illnesses.
One common diagnosis?
German measles!
Bispebjerg Hospital
was to provide
sanctuary to nearly
two thousand Jews
during the rescue effort.

Leo Goldberger, a teenager,
spent that first night
with his family
as the guests of wealthy Jews
living on the coast.

To our chagrin, the family took off for
Sweden during the night without even
telling us or their . . . maid.

Nine-year-old Mette Shayne
hid first at their neighbors',
then at her father's colleague's,
then at a farm,
then in a forest,
then at a children's camp,
then in a hotel,
then in the bushes on the beach
waiting for their boat.

Baruch Griegst
and his son, Arie,
had planned their escape
on a large boat
with other Jews.
But their bus had a flat tire
on the way there
and the ship sailed without them.

It seemed like bad luck,
but in a twist of fate,
they later discovered
that the ship and all aboard
were captured
by the Nazis.
That flat tire had saved their lives.

NOT ALL ESCAPED

Some Jews were discovered
outside of Copenhagen.
They had missed the warning.
Others had simply not believed it:
this couldn't happen in Denmark!

Two hundred and two elderly people
living in the Jewish Home for the Aged,
the Krystalgade Nursing Home,
were captured in Copenhagen.
They were taken to a ship
called the *Wartheland*
on Langelinie Quay.
The prisoners were bound
for Theresienstadt,
a concentration camp
in German-occupied Czechoslovakia,
now the Czech Republic.

One witness reported,

> *It was terrible to see old people . . . lying*
> *there, wailing and crying. An elderly*
> *lady, unable to walk, had been placed on a*

mattress and lifted onboard with a crane.
She was in great pain.

Such cruelty!
Unthinkable.
    Unbearable.
        Unforgivable.

OCTOBER 2

The German ship *Wartheland*
deporting the captured Jews
set sail on October 2.
With a capacity of five thousand people,
it left the dock with only 202 Jews
and 150 Danish Communists aboard.

Another eighty-two Jews
arrested outside of the city
boarded three of the forty
freight train cars.

In all, the Nazis
eventually deported

about 470 Jews to the
Theresienstadt
concentration camp,
including Jews
who were captured in later days.
About 101 were not Danish citizens,
but Jewish refugees
living in Denmark.

The great majority of Jews
had not been caught.

JUDENREIN

The roundup had failed.
Miserably.

And yet, Werner Best,
the Nazi behind the roundup,
put his best spin on the news.
He telegraphed Berlin
on October 2, boasting:
mission accomplished.

Denmark was Judenrein—
cleansed of Jews.

The truth was
they weren't gone;
they were in hiding
at neighbors' houses,
in summer homes,
in stables,
in hospital wards,
in churches,
in cellars,
in attics,
in warehouses,
in the woods.
            Waiting for help.

PART XIII

Stowaways

ENOUGH!

Smell the smoke of democracy dying
Taste the bile of the Nazis lying
Feel the fight in no longer complying
See the Resistance electrifying!
Hear the shouts of the Danish crying—
Enough!
       Enough!
              Enough!

SCAPEGOATS

To the Danish public,
the Nazis blamed the Jews
for terror and sabotage.
Now that they were "gone,"
the "model protectorate"
could go back to law and order.

Nazis announced
that Danish soldiers
held captive
under martial law

would be released.
The Nazis said,

> *the Jews have been removed from public life*
> *and prevented from continuing to poison*
> *the atmosphere.*

The Danish people knew better.
They were outraged.

PROTESTS

The Danish people
voiced their fury.

> *At least forty protests [poured in from]*
> *judges, lawyers, teachers, engineers,*
> *officials, police, the army and navy,*
> *libraries and museums, . . . trade unions*
> *and the Supreme Court.*

On October 3,
Lutheran ministers read
a letter of protest

in churches
around the nation
that said,

> *Every man has a value in the eyes of*
> *God. . . . Whenever Jews are persecuted*
> *because of their religion or race, it is the*
> *duty of the Christian church to protest. . . .*
> *We shall fight for the cause that our Jewish*
> *brothers and sisters may preserve the same*
> *freedom . . . we ourselves value more highly*
> *than life itself.*

The Danish Freedom Council
called upon every Dane
to help any Jewish people
still in hiding.

Hitler and Adolf Eichmann
(the SS chief in charge of
"the Final Solution")
were furious.
Eichmann later said,

> *The result was meager. . . . I had to recall*
> *my transports—it was for me a mighty*
> *disgrace.*

But both the Nazis
and the Danes knew
the Jews couldn't
stay in hiding for long.

GETTING STARTED

Henny and *Gerda III*
began their rescue operation
right away.
She and the lighthouse crew
conducted their first evacuation
in the early morning hours
of the roundup.
They continued to sail
ten to fifteen people
to safety each day after that.

For weeks,
Henny sneaked out
of the house at one a.m.

> *Father and Mother never said*
> *anything . . . when I went at night, nor*

when I came home in the morning. Poor
Mother. To get out of the house, I had to go
through her bedroom. It probably wasn't
pleasant for her, she heard me every night
sneak out, but she climbed deeper under the
pillows, and pretended as if nothing was
going on. Thank you to Mother.

The crew's biggest problem
was locating their passengers.
Their Jewish friends
and neighbors
were nowhere to be found.
Henny said,

I knew a lot of Jews and the four men on
[Gerda III] knew a lot of Jews. And we
had to find [them], which sometimes was
very difficult because they [were] hiding.

They had to be careful
because asking around
could tip off Nazi informants
and sink the whole operation.
Henny said,

Just one wrong person's knowledge about
Gerda III *[and] its route, and it would*
be spoiled forever, and the Lighthouse
[Buoy] and Supply Company would be in a
terrible awkward situation.

It could compromise
her father's standing
in the navy.

So at first Henny relied on the
Gerda III crew and the men's
families and neighbors
in their hometown—
a small, tight-knit
fishing village called Dragør,
about eleven kilometers south
of Copenhagen.

Drogden Lighthouse keeper
Ejler Haubirk Sr.
was from Dragør;
as an early Resistance fighter,
his home quickly became a shelter
for Jews on the run.
He and his sons enlisted

Dragør fishermen,
such as Godtfred Lundquist
and his son Kaj,
to aid the evacuation.
Many others
joined the cause,
hiding Jews in their houses
or ferrying them across the strait.

Word spread.
Henny said,

> *As soon as you got hold of one or two*
> *[Jewish] families, they always knew where*
> *you could get hold of other families.*

FREEDOM FOR A FEE?

Many fishermen
charged a fee for their services.
The costs ranged in price
and were highest during
the first hectic days of the
evacuation.

*Prices per person varied from 1,000 to
about 10,000 kroner.*

Some families
paid up to 50,000 kroner,
up to 100,000 kroner,
at a time when "the monthly
salary for a fully trained worker
was 414 kroner."

Extra funding was sorely needed.
Some people mortgaged their houses.
The underground movement
sought donations,
raised funds to help,
and worked to discourage
profiteers.

To be fair, the fishermen
were mostly poor
and they were risking everything.
They could lose their boats,
their livelihoods,
        even their lives.
Their boats could be stopped
by German patrols,
blown up by mines

planted in the harbor,
or confiscated by the Nazis
upon their return.
It could cost 15,000 to 30,000 kroner
to replace a fishing boat.

Drogden Lighthouse keeper
Ingolf Haubrick said,

> *The wealthier of the refugees paid for those
> who could not afford the price. . . . No one
> who could not afford the price was left
> behind.*

There were occasionally
kind souls who

> *were paid with a bottle of Snaps* [sic] *or a
> bicycle.*

And there were others
who did not charge a fee,
people like Henny
and her friends on *Gerda III.*
Already paid to sail
by the Lighthouse Authority,

they had no need
to charge the refugees.

Regardless of the fee,
skippers and crew lent a hand
at great risk to themselves.
Their families could be left bereft
and penniless.
Fees were insurance
against disaster.
        And disasters did happen.

Eight boats from the small coastal village
of Snekkersten successfully evacuated
refugees to Sweden on October 4.
But upon their return the Gestapo
was lying in wait.
Seven boats were captured
and twelve fishermen
were imprisoned.
Only one boat and one skipper escaped.

"A SMALL DUNKIRK"

Despite the risks,
people all over Denmark
stepped up
to answer the call for help.
More than six hundred vessels—
canoes, rowboats, sailboats,
kayaks, fishing boats,
speedboats, patrol boats—
set out to make
the dangerous trip
across the strait to Sweden.
Henny said,

> *We did not think too much about any*
> *risk. . . . we never knew if today would be*
> *the last day in our lives. It was the right*
> *thing to do, so we did it. Simple as that!*

An Olympic oarsman
named Knud Christiansen
put his athletic prowess to use.
He had seen the Nazis in action
during the 1936 Olympics
in Berlin.

So in 1943,
he took it upon himself to row
one Jew at a time
across the Øresund
in his Olympic racing boat
despite the freezing temperatures
of October, November,
and December.

Boats, big and small,
departed from more than
fifty places along the coast
for a voyage that ranged from
three to twenty-four kilometers.

The trip could take forty minutes,
but usually it took about two hours . . .
if nothing went wrong.

> *If German patrol boats turned up, the*
> *vessels had to do some fishing to avoid*
> *arousing suspicions and that could make*
> *the journey much longer.*

For the Jews hidden under nets
or in holds below deck,

those hours circled
round and round
like the hands on
an everlasting clock
spinning out to kingdom come.

PART XIV

Mates

CHANGING COURSE

For Jørgen, Mix,
and their group,
the news of the roundup
had put ideas of sabotage
on hold.
Now nothing mattered
but saving the Jews.

Jørgen said,

> *[when] the official message of the pogroms*
> *was sent out . . . the outrage and despair*
> *knew no limit.*

> *[The] long discussions in our apartment*
> *between the pacifists and the activists . . .*
> *stopped. . . . There was no question any*
> *longer of passive resistance. . . . active*
> *resistance was the only way out.*

> *We got together in our little apartment on*
> *Saturday, [the day after] the persecution.*
> *Then the first thing to do was . . . to get*
> *hold of money [to] be able to pay for the*
> *transport across the Sound.*

FINDING FUNDS

Jørgen's sister Elsebet
and a friend
took off that weekend
to visit wealthy estate owners
outside of Copenhagen
looking for donations for the cause.
They visited
a baroness,
a count,
and crashed an elegant dinner party.
Impressed with the
young people's naivete,
idealism, and spirit,
everyone gave freely.

Jørgen explained,

> *The financial problems were solved within*
> *forty-eight hours. When they returned,*
> *they had one million Danish kroner, a*
> *considerable fortune. Additional funds*
> *were raised by other members of our group*
> *and many refugees were also able to make*
> *significant contributions.*

ENLISTING BOATS

With money,
it wasn't difficult to
approach the fishermen.
Ebba Lund,
a twenty-year-old girl
in Jørgen's group,
went to friends she had met
on family vacations.

Jørgen said,

> She knew all the fishermen . . . [She] asked,
> "Will you be ready to take Jews across and
> will you be willing to ask your colleagues
> to do the same? We are ready to pay for
> this." . . . They were willing, and I believe
> she got . . . [a] little fleet [of] about ten
> fishing boats.

Ebba set up an escape route
from Skudehavnen
(a northern port of Copenhagen)
to Barsebäckshamn, Sweden.

FINDING THE JEWS

With money and boats,
Jørgen's group was ready!
Jørgen said,

> [Our] main problem was really to find the
> Jews, . . . but eventually we found them
> in the backyards, we found them in the
> forests outside Copenhagen, and then they
> found us.

Word went around
that Jews could find rescue
by finding Ebba Lund
and her bright red hat.

THE RED CAP GIRL

A red beret
was a signal, a sign,
like a blaze in the forest,
a trusty trail marker for Jews
pursued by Nazi packs.

Find the young woman
who wore it,
code name
"Little Red Riding Hood."
Ebba Lund
would show you a path
out of the woods.

RESCUE UNDER WAY

Jørgen's parents
sent him their first Jewish couple.
Ebba remembered,

> *the first people I arranged transport for
> were two Czech Jews . . . [It] must have
> taken place either Monday, October 4, or
> the next day.*

Meanwhile,
on the other side of Copenhagen,
Henny and *Gerda III*'s rescue
was well under way.

Henny said,

> *A hectic time started. . . . a dreadful
> [number of Jews] . . . needed to get to the
> other side of the Sound as soon as possible.*

But Henny needed help—
a larger network
to find the refugees.

And she was determined
to do more
to fight the Nazis, too.
How could she connect with
like-minded Resistance fighters?

> *Getting into the Resistance movement*
> *was very difficult. I mean, you didn't*
> *put an announcement in the newspaper*
> *saying, "I'd like to go join the Resistance*
> *movement." You had to be asked by*
> *somebody and as nobody trusted nobody*
> *[sic], . . . it was very difficult for people to*
> *pick people for the movement.*

Once again, mutual friends
were the key.

The crew of *Gerda III*
would lead Henny to Mix,
who in turn
would lead her to Jørgen.

A GIRL THEY COULD TRUST

No one knows
the exact date
Henny and Mix first met.
They might have seen
each other around the
naval dockyards.

Jørgen had asked Mix
to recruit a young woman
to help with surveillance.
He knew that
a man and woman
walking together,
pretending to be in love,
could scout an area
without arousing
too much suspicion.

Mix went to the crew
of *Gerda III*.
He asked them,

> *Do you know a girl . . . we could trust?*

The crew recommended Henny
without hesitation.
Henny remembered:

> *Mix looked me up one day out on Holmen,*
> *sometime in the beginning of October.*
> *He was a young, dynamic navy cadet,*
> *and everything he undertook had to go fast.*

Surely, they discussed
the rescue,
but Mix also mentioned
other work.

> *For a long time we walked and talked*
> *together . . . and he told me a little about*
> *what the work was going to be. Mix did*
> *not hide that the work was dangerous and*
> *suggested that I take my time giving him*
> *an answer. There was no reason for me to*
> *wait because of course I wanted to join.*

WIN-WIN

Mix introduced Henny
to Jørgen, who was impressed
with her efforts.

> *[She] had been active with the transports of*
> *Jews to Sweden, independent of ourselves.*

Henny offered
Gerda III's help.
A win-win!
Jørgen's group would get
a second escape route;
Henny would get help
locating escapees.

Jørgen said,

> *Through their personal contacts, two*
> *young girls, Ebba Lund and Henny*
> *Sinding, who had joined our group, . . .*
> *we established two important escape routes*
> *from Copenhagen. Finding Jews, bringing*
> *them to the harbor, and organizing and*
> *protecting their embarkation became our*

most important tasks during the following
weeks. Ebba and Henny were always there
to see [the refugees] on board.

BOOKING ESCAPE

Henny, Ebba, Mix, and Jørgen
also depended on
other friends
to find the Jews.

One was Dr. Køster,
head surgeon
of Bispebjerg Hospital,
who organized the rescue efforts
of his staff.

Another source was
twenty-eight-year-old
Mogens Staffeldt,
who ran the Nordic Bookstore.
He printed books
banned by the Nazis

in the center of Copenhagen,
right across from Nazi headquarters.
He delighted in operating
right under the Nazis' noses.

Mogens heard about
the coming roundup
from a sea captain,
one of many Germans
who disapproved
of this persecution.
Mogens instantly
turned his bookstore
into another front
for coordinating
escape operations.

Mogens told his staff,

For the next fourteen days we don't sell books,
we make a travel agency here instead.

Mogens would place
a book by Danish pastor
and playwright Kaj Munk
in the window.

It was a signal that
it was safe for Jews to enter.
But typically Jews
sent a non-Jewish friend
to the store to arrange passage.
Mogens would give them the date
and place to meet.

THE WHEELS IN MOTION

With money, boats, and contacts,
Jørgen said,

> *Word by word, mouth by mouth, we were*
> *known.*

Mogens and others
would supply
the names of Jews.

Then some of Jørgen's group,
Henny, and the *Gerda III* crew
would arrange safe houses

for the refugees
near the northern harbor
and near Henny's warehouse.
Some safe houses had guests
for more than a week;
Henny did the math
of which fifteen would go when.
Henny said,

> *We had to divide them into teams to make*
> *sure that children and parents were brought*
> *over together.*

At preappointed times,
Henny and Jørgen's sisters
would spring into action
from their different locations.

Jørgen's sisters would
escort Jews
to the harbor
where they would connect
with "Little Red Riding Hood."
Ebba Lund would see them
onto the boats.
Ebba said,

*You had to do it in daytime. We had a
curfew. You could go to prison just for being
outside.*

Ebba took care of the payments
to the fishing captains.

*I always paid half of their money that we
agreed upon before they went out. [Once]
they could report that everything was well
and the people were [safe], then they got the
other half of the money.*

Fishing boats were allowed
to set out at night
because their catch was
an important food source.

*October was peak season for herring
[fishing], which is why the many
nocturnal trips didn't arouse suspicion.*

Gerda III was scheduled to
leave at seven a.m. each day,
so Henny had
a more dangerous job,

escorting Jews at night.
Henny knew taking this risk—
breaking curfew—
was madness. She said,

> *It was completely crazy. . . . It was a*
> *testament to how young and inexperienced—*
> *yes, even foolhardy—we were.*

If they were caught out after curfew,
they would all be arrested.
    It was a chance they had to take.

OFF THE BEACH, INTO THE BREACH

Day and night,
for the next few weeks,
Ebba and Henny
launched their boats
into the breach.
Henny said,

> *It was exhilarating!*

She liked being part
of Jørgen's team—
the togetherness of the group.
She felt excitement
and camaraderie,
along with a renewed
sense of purpose.
What could go wrong?

PART XV

Smuggler

SO MANY LIVES, SO MANY STORIES

The Jews seeking salvation
in Sweden
were as different
as people can be.
Some were infants in arms;
some, elderly on their last legs.
Some were able-bodied,
stouthearted, thick-skinned,
but all shouldered
an impossible burden
of worry and sorrow.

Some were landowners,
suddenly homeless.
Some were executives,
suddenly unemployed.
Some were shopkeepers,
suddenly out of business.
Some were schoolchildren,
suddenly dismissed.

Some looked forward
to safety ahead;
others looked back
to the lives they'd led.

Each one had a story to tell.
This is Aron's.

IMAGINE

Fourteen-year-old Aron,
his parents, and
four younger brothers and sisters
faced double the danger.
They were not only Jewish,
but also Danish Communists.
They were warned
of the upcoming Nazi roundup
by the manager
of their apartment building.

Imagine getting
that knock on the door.
Imagine being told you had to leave . . .
Now!
Where would you go?
    What would you take?
        What would you need?
Warm clothing?

Money?
  Your keys?
    Your ID?
      Food?

Carrying suitcases
would give you away.
Better to pack a school bag or
a shopping bag instead.

What would you leave behind?
When would you be back?
    If ever?
No time to think.
Time to go.
    Now!

Imagine the bravery
of the manager
who offered Aron's family
shelter in her own apartment
that night.
Imagine her courage.
Imagine knowing
you could be killed
    for your kindness.

KEEP MOVING

It wasn't safe to stay
in the manager's apartment
for too long.
The next day,
the Engelhardt family
had to separate,
going into hiding
in four different homes.
Aron stayed with
his father's colleague,
along with his
eight-year-old brother, Rudi.
They were often left home alone
when the couple went to work.
Days went by.
Days of isolation,
    of questions.
What would happen
to them?
Would they ever
see their family again?
Days of anxiety and fear
alternating with boredom.
Days of getting on
each other's nerves.

THE BOY WHO CRIED WOLF

Rudi liked to tease Aron,
as siblings do.

> *Sometimes he would go to the window and*
> *say, "Aron, the Germans are coming" and*
> *then I would sprint to the window and he*
> *[would] laugh.*

One morning
the boys had just
woken up
and Rudi did it again.
"The Germans are coming!"
he said.
"Ah, stop that nonsense,"
replied Aron.
But Rudi started to cry.
Aron went
to the window.

> *True enough, a German military vehicle*
> *was parked right below our windows and*
> *two men in uniform [walked] up the stairs*
> *and [rang] the doorbell.*

The boys sneaked out
to the door and listened.
Their father had said
that he and the Resistance fighters
might come for them
dressed as Germans.
Rudi whispered,

>*We better open the door, otherwise we
won't make it to Sweden.*

Aron clapped his hand
over Rudi's mouth.

>*I was too afraid to open the door . . . I had
a bad feeling something was wrong because
my father wasn't with them. . . . We heard
someone coming out, . . . the neighbor, who
told them nobody was home. . . . They
[walked] down the stairs again . . . [got]
into their cars and [drove] away.*

Aron's father came to
get them half an hour later.
Their visitors
had indeed been Nazis!

ON THE MOVE AGAIN

Aron's father
had received word:
pick up your family,
take them to
Bispebjerg Hospital,
where Dr. Køster
was organizing rescue operations.
They were told:
Go to the hospital's chapel by nine a.m.
Pretend you're attending a funeral.
From there, you'll be taken
to the boats.

Aron's family arrived
at the hospital
on October 7.
Aron remembered,

> *We were dropped off at the entrance to*
> *the crematorium . . . a bit . . . a bit scary,*
> *you know.*

They were led
down, down, down

to the basement
where they found
many other Jews—
whole families—
waiting in silence,
waiting for their escape.
The Engelhardts
joined them,
waiting all that day.
Plans had been made
to evacuate 40 Jews.
At least 140 people showed up
that first morning,
with more and more arriving
all through the day.

Aron said,

> We were told that we would be going to
> the northern coast, Snekkersten . . . But
> then later, they came back to us and told
> us, "It's not possible, there are too many
> German patrols on the roads, you'll have
> to stay the night here, and then we'll
> see tomorrow. . . ." We were scared. I
> remember my dad started to cry, it was the

first time I had ever seen him cry. He was
scared it would all fall apart now.

Where would the staff
hide so many overnight?
Where would they sleep?
What would they eat?

The doctors and nurses
dove into action.
By ten p.m. that night,
many of the Jews
were given hospital beds,
complete with phony names
on bogus medical charts.
Aron and his family
were hidden
in the nurses' quarters.

They got a couple of hours' sleep,
but then were awakened,
told they were leaving
that night after all.
Aron's family was escorted
downstairs to an ambulance.

It drove through the city, not north.
Nobody knew where we were going. I
wasn't that scared. . . . I felt somewhat
safe . . . that we were in capable hands and
these people [knew] what they were doing.

CAPABLE HANDS

The ambulance
dropped Aron's family
at a dark dock
in Christianshavn,
where Henny and her friends
took over.
They escorted them,
two by two,
to Hans Just's warehouse,
near where *Gerda III*
was docked.

Getting to the warehouse
was a dangerous
stage of the rescue.

They were out in the open,
in the dark streets
after curfew.
    It was verboten.

TO THE WAREHOUSE

Hearts racing,
barely breathing,
Aron and his family
followed along.
Later, Henny said,

> *Incredibly, we were lucky enough to never
> meet Germans on Strandgade at night.
> The refugees spent the night in the attic
> of the warehouse. We had a lot of trouble
> getting them to understand that they had
> to be completely quiet. It was even worse
> when we had small children with us, not
> to mention babies. We always had sleeping
> pills with us and almost every night it was
> necessary to give the children a pill.*

Aron's four-year-old sister, Nina,
was given a pill that night
so she wouldn't cry out.
Henny offered the others food.
She said,

> *There was always something to eat or*
> *drink for our "guests" in the attic, but no*
> *one could eat, we all had a bad case of*
> *stomachache, and the night seemed endlessly*
> *long.*

THE GERMAN PATROL

Henny said her biggest headache
was the German patrol,
two guards
who marched back and forth
outside the warehouse.

When it was time,
the *Gerda III* crew
would signal to Henny
to start boarding

the passengers.
Henny led them
downstairs,
lined them up, and
instructed them to run
to the boat,
one by one.

They had to dash
the few meters to the boat
while the German guards'
backs were turned.

> *It was nervewrecking* [sic] *because it . . .*
> *depended on using the opportunity, every*
> *time they . . . turned around, and were*
> *walking away from each other.*

The crew helped them
onboard and stashed them
in the cargo hold.

> *When all the adults were onboard, [I]*
> *brought the children. It could take quite*
> *a long time to get everyone onboard, close*
> *the lid to the cargo, and gather a lot of*

material over the lid. It is unbelievable
that the Germans never turned around
to look.

Aron remembered,

> *One by one we were brought on the*
> *boat. . . . Mom, Nina, Sima, and I came*
> *into the small crew cabin [below the bow]*
> *along with a few others. There was a very*
> *nervous man smoking cigarettes. . . . My*
> *father, Rudi, and Miriam were put into*
> *the cargo hold. Suddenly, I heard a child*
> *crying and a baby was handed down to*
> *me. . . . I cradled the child and it* [sic]
> *calmed down.*

ONE LAST HURDLE

Once the small group
of refugees were well hidden
in the hold,
Gerda III was ready to depart.

Henny remembered
one more hurdle:

> *We all said a silent prayer, because at the*
> *very moment [the crew] started the motor,*
> *the two guards came running. Every*
> *morning they had to come onboard to check*
> *that everything was in order.*

Aron's family, hidden away, heard

> *the tramp of boots on the deck*
> *and the sound of German voices.*

After all their days of hiding,
close calls and quick escapes,
there were Nazis centimeters away.
Would they catch them this time?
Henny said,

> *Either they were nice Germans, or they*
> *were very sleepy, because they never*
> *thought of asking to remove the things over*
> *the lid to see what was hidden in the cargo.*
> *The crew was also very quick to offer them*
> *a [drink], . . . that they probably needed*

after having walked up and down the quay
the whole night.

This is how Gerda III *was sneaked to the*
sea, officially to Drogden Lighthouse, but
on the way it went over to the Swedish
coast, got the refugees safely onto shore, and
thereafter set sail for Drogden.

NAVIGATING A COURSE

Gerda III's Captain Tønnesen
had different routes
he could take to Sweden.
Leaving the dock,
he could decide
to go north on
the Københavns Havn waterway.
The advantage?
This route was the shortest distance
to Sweden.
The disadvantage?
This route led past the king's castle

and the Holmen Naval Yard,
both overrun with Nazis.

The alternative route
was to turn south,
where only smaller boats
could travel.
They could reach the Øresund
going around Amager's shore,
heading to Malmö,
Limhamn, Klagshamn, or Skanör.

The captain's decision
for each trip
depended on the weather,
the currents,
and the German patrols.

Gerda III was fairly safe
if she was en route
to the Drogden Lighthouse.
Daily supply trips there
was her job after all.
If hailed by German patrol boats,
the captain could simply
tell the Nazis that *Gerda* was

the lighthouse cutter, doing what it had
been ordered to do.

But the trip to Skanör,
which was
at least two hours
from the Danish coast,
took *Gerda* way off course.
Highly suspicious.
Dangerous waters, indeed!

TO SWEDEN?

Aron said that
Gerda III sailed out
into the harbor
and turned south.
They passed
"under the Knippelsbro Bridge
and then under the Langebro Bridge."
Through a slit in the hatch,
he saw "German soldiers
patrolling the bridges,"

looking down at *Gerda III*
as she motored by.
She had seven kilometers
to go to the channel
and five and a half more kilometers
to the sea.
There they would have to brave
twenty-eight more kilometers
of October's wild winds
and whitecap waves
to reach their destination in Sweden.

As Henny watched them leave,
she had to wonder:
Would Aron and his family
make it safely across?

Henny didn't know.
She had done her part
and now there were
others who needed her.

> *I stood in the warehouse and saw the cutter*
> *set sail, then I went home in the early*
> *morning hour.*

Later that night
Henny would sneak out again.
There were others she must help.
    Others like Gerd Lilienfeldt.

GERD'S STORY

Gerd was a Jewish boy
born in Germany,
who had come to Denmark
in his mid-teens
as part of the
Youth Aliyah group—
a last possible way
out of Nazi Germany.
He and several hundred
other Jewish teenagers
traveled there
to study agriculture
before going to live
permanently in Palestine.

The Nazi occupation
in Denmark
put an end to those plans.
The route to Palestine
was cut off by the Germans
and in the next few years,
Gerd lost all contact with
the family he had left behind
in Germany.

As luck would have it,
nineteen-year-old Gerd
was not at home
when the Nazis tried
to round up the Jews
on October 1.
As he later told his son,
he was in hiding,
suspecting something awful
was about to happen.
On his own,
he made his way
to Gilleleje,
a small town
in northern Denmark
(a community that would succeed

in evacuating 20 percent
of escaping Jews).
There, he would try to board
a fishing boat for Sweden.

Even careful plans
often went awry.
When the Gestapo arrived
at the harbor,
a Resistance group
hid Gerd and others
in the attic loft of
the Gilleleje Church
on the night of October 6.
Through the small round window,
they could see Sweden
across the waters,
their freedom within reach,
less than an hour away.

The Gilleleje Resistance leaders
reassured the terrified Jews
that they had a plan.

They would set off
a false air-raid siren,

pretending British warplanes
had been spotted.
The Gestapo
would run for cover!
That siren would be the
signal for the Jews
to head for the boats.

The siren never went off.
All thanks to a stikker,
an informant.

A NAZI SPY

The rumor was
that a local woman
in love with a Nazi
betrayed them.
She supposedly noticed Jews
shepherded into the church
and called
Gestapo chief Hans Juhl,
in Helsingør,
the man ultimately responsible

for half of the arrests
that were made
after the October 1 roundup.

After the war,
this woman was tried
and found *not* guilty.
No one knows who the
informant was.
But the tip-off meant trouble
all the same.

IN THE CHURCH ATTIC

The refugees sat,
silent as church mice,
and waited.

> They [listened] to the tick-tock from the
> [church] clock—minute after minute,
> hour after hour. Some [said] it was like a
> heartbeat.

Like their own hearts pounding.

One man
checked the window
from time to time.
Late that night he saw

> *a sight that made him hold his breath—*
> *groups of German soldiers . . . setting up*
> *machine guns on the church lawn.*

At midnight, Gestapo chief Juhl
surrounded the church
with heavily armed troops
and pounded on the door,
threatening to shoot
if it wasn't opened.
Tense hours passed.
Juhl wasn't
breaking down the door,
but he wasn't leaving either.

At three a.m., Juhl woke
church gravedigger Jørgensen
and demanded the spare key
for the church.

The terrified Jews
were forced to give themselves up.

"Not me," said a boy
named Bruno,
who climbed into the bell tower
and hid there.

Gerd followed!

> *I tried getting to the roof, but it was
> impossible. When the Germans found me
> up in the tower, they started jabbing me
> with their bayonets and I crawled down
> again. I was the last one to be captured.*

He and his fellow Jews
were herded
at gunpoint
onto German trucks,
then slammed
behind bars
in the nearby
Horserød Prison.
Next stop?
Theresienstadt concentration camp.

THE BELL TOWER BOY

Helpers found the boy
who had escaped
from the church attic
the next morning
"more dead than alive."
He and nine other people
tried to row to Sweden
a few days later.
Not far from shore,
their rowboat capsized
and Bruno,
like many who tried to escape,
met his fate
in the cold Øresund sea.

It was a risk so many took
to escape the Nazis.
Many succeeded.
But at least twenty-two people
and probably many more
drowned.
Just like Bruno.

TO PRISON

Gerd and about eighty others
had spent the night
in Denmark's Horserød Prison.
When morning dawned,
Nazis started to load them
on a truck headed
to the harbor,
where a ship bound for
a concentration camp
awaited.
But Gerd was still looking
for a way out.

Gerd had had tuberculosis
and he knew the Germans
were terrified of catching
the highly infectious disease.
He simulated a coughing fit,
a TB attack,
which made his nose bleed
to the horror of the German guards.
They hurried him off
to a different open bed truck
where he wouldn't
infect everyone.

Along the road,
the truck stopped
and Gerd saw his chance
to make his getaway.
He jumped off.

> *I ran away from there and I was lucky that*
> *at the same moment a taxi drove by. The*
> *driver quickly opened the door for me and*
> *drove away. I have no idea if there was*
> *any shooting or yelling after me. . . . You*
> *just run.*

The taxi driver spirited him off
to Øresundshospitalet.
The doctor in charge
took him home and hid him
for a few days
until he could arrange passage
on a boat.
      On Henny's boat.

Henny met Gerd
in the early morning hours
of October 15
the same way she met so many others:

in the dark of night,
leading him to the warehouse.

Gerd remembered
the tension
inside the warehouse.
He and the others
cowered in the shadows.
Henny tried to calm them,
but it wasn't easy.
Most were petrified.
Gerd said,

> *In a situation like that, you are completely*
> *alone and totally dependent on help.*

GERD'S JOURNEY

The next morning
when it was time,
Henny signaled Gerd
to run.
He said,

I darted across the quay . . . and was practically thrown into the boat. It all happened very quickly.

The trip to Sweden
usually took a few hours,
but to Gerd it felt like
"an eternity."

I was lying in the cargo with a small child on top of me. The boat rolled and the child had to throw up constantly. But I just kept on holding them [sic] tight to me. It must have been a coping reaction.

SUCCESS!

Gerd and Aron
both made it to Sweden.
Aron and his family arrived
safely in southern Skanör;
Gerd in northern Barsebäckshamn.

Gerd remembered his arrival.

*Someone opened the hatch and said, "we
are in Sweden." It was not until I came out
into the quay and saw the Swedish police
officers that I dared believe it. Then I felt
a sense of relief, such an enormous sense
of relief. I did not think to thank the crew
and when I turned around to look after
the boat, it was already leaving the harbor
again.*

There were others
anxiously waiting
for their turn to escape
on *Gerda III.*

OVER AND OVER

Gerd and Aron were just two
of at least three hundred Jews
that Henny and *Gerda III*
helped to escape.
Henny wrote that the operation was
"every night, many weeks in a row."

Over and over,
that October, *Gerda III*
made the dangerous trip to Sweden
more than twenty times.
Over and over,
Henny replayed the same scene,
day in and day out—
sneaking out at one a.m.,
escorting traumatized Jews
to the warehouse,
hiding until dawn's light
signaled time to run to the boat.
Delivering sedated children.
Over and over,
watching as the Nazis
conducted their morning inspections.
Going home to sleep a bit
before sneaking out again that night.
Over and over,
rescue drove her.
Until success!
    It was over.

LOOKING THE OTHER WAY

There is evidence
that some Germans
didn't see eye to eye
with their superiors
on the persecution of the Jews.

In hindsight,
some modern historians
believe that after the initial roundup,
German forces would
look the other way
to keep up "their fiction
of a peaceful occupation"
or deliver the rescuers
to the Danish police
for a mild punishment.

After the mass raids on the 1st of October,
follow-up searches were left in the hands
of a small group of Gestapo officers in
Copenhagen and Helsingør. Covering
the whole of the Øresund strait between
Denmark and Sweden effectively was an
impossible task for such a small group.

Some historians say
Wehrmacht military units
preferred to set their sights on
"rooting out Danish spies
and naval coast guard staff
who were working against them."
More than Jews, they wanted
to spot boats
suspected of transporting
saboteurs, weapons,
or secret intelligence.
Some boats, like *Gerda III*, did all three.

The threat of danger,
of death,
of imprisonment,
of deportation to
a concentration camp,
hung over everyone
who crossed the Øresund.

Often fate came down to
the luck of the draw—
who saw you,
who stopped you,
and when.

Ulrich Plesner
told of his neighbor Ole
ferrying a boatload
of Danish Jews
who were hidden in the fish hold.
Ole's boat was stopped by
a German navy patrol.

> *The German captain shouted, "What are
> you carrying?" And Ole shouted back,
> "Fish." The captain then jumped onto
> the deck, leaving his crew to cover him,
> and demanded that the hatches to the fish
> hold be removed. He stared a long time
> at several dozen frightened people looking
> up at him. Finally, he turned and said to
> Ole, in a loud voice that could be heard
> by his own crew as well: "Ah, fish!" Then
> he returned to his boat and sailed into the
> night.*

When stopped,
boat captains had no way of
knowing whether they would face
threats, ambivalence, or kindness.
All they knew was that their efforts

to help the Jews were risky,
they could mean life or death
in the blink of an eye.
        They did it anyway.

THE VIEW FROM SWEDEN

An eyewitness account
in a Swedish newspaper
described the Swedes'
reaction to the arrival
of the boats.

> *We are standing on the beach, watching
> the dark water. . . . We were waiting for
> hours. Will anybody cross tonight? . . .
> Suddenly you hear a throbbing from
> somewhere, the sound of a motor. Clunk-
> clunk. Slowly the boat approaches, the
> pale faces of the passengers . . . look like
> ghosts . . . The darkness envelops all but
> their white, upturned . . . expressive faces,
> some petrified, some . . . suffering, and*

some radiant with happiness. But on the faces . . . you read fatigue, a bottomless feeling of fatigue and resignation coupled with traces of fear. . . . Suddenly someone on board starts singing "Du gamla, du fria" (the Swedish national anthem). And everybody joins. . . . It's almost more than you can bear. Tears run down the cheeks of tall, hefty men standing on the beach watching. . . . A Jew kneels and kisses the soil of Sweden.

MISSION ACCOMPLISHED

Henny and her fellow Danes
had done their jobs.
Refugee Herbert Pundik said,

> *The Danes saved the Jews. And this, in turn, [saved] the self-respect of the Danes.*

Together,
astonishingly,

they helped
7,742 of Denmark's 8,250 Jews
take flight,
plus 686 non-Jewish family members.
Some 1,376 were "stateless Jews"
who had been
refugees from Germany
living in Denmark.
Jørgen and Ebba's fleet
of about thirteen boats
helped more than
eight hundred people flee.

"Few boats, if any, evacuated as many people"
as Henny and the crew of *Gerda III*—
about three hundred souls.

But there was more work . . .
        much more dangerous work to be done.

PART XVI

All Hands on Deck

DAWNING

The persecution of the Jews
was an awakening
for many Danes.
Those who had tried
to stay out of the fight
joined the Resistance in droves.
Aage Bertelsen,
a schoolteacher,
echoed the voice of many
when he said,

> The dark night of the first and second of
> October [was] a personal dawn. . . . In the
> face of these open acts of atrocity, . . . action
> was the word . . . No honest man could
> possibly refrain from action after this raid,
> when the persecuted cried for help.

The Danish police
stopped cooperating
with the Germans,
stopped obeying orders.

> It took a long time before it dawned on
> the authority-minded Germans that the

Danish police could deviate from laws and
regulations and act on their own initiative,
guided by their conviction alone.

Now the Danish police
aided the Resistance.
Sabotage increased.
So did retaliation.

THE SITUATION BLOWS UP

Demonstrations
led to altercations
led to incriminations
led to condemnations
led to retaliations
led to assassinations.

FURY

Exploding with anger
about the ever frequent
acts of sabotage,
Hitler retaliated
against the
Danish Resistance
with murder.

The renowned Danish poet,
playwright, and pastor Kaj Munk
was the first person
assassinated as payback.
It was no longer enough
to execute saboteurs.
Hitler commanded five Danes
be killed for every German soldier
or informant who died.

Just when the Danes thought
things couldn't get much worse,
                            they did.
The Nazis had to be stopped.

CARRYING ON

Now that most of the Jews
had escaped,
meetings in
Jørgen Kieler's apartment
turned to sabotage
once again.

When approached
in mid-October
to help start an offshoot
of Holger Danske,
Jørgen readily agreed.
Holger Danske 2
would carry on
the sabotage work
of Holger Danske,
whose leaders had been forced
to evacuate to Sweden.
Jørgen gathered
a core group—his siblings,
his cousin, his classmates,
Mix, and other naval cadets
whom Mix had recruited.

*On October 14, the naval cadets were
released from Holmen and eleven of them
immediately joined our sabotage group,
which was now ready for action at last.*

At the time,
"sabotage was considered a man's job,"
but Jørgen notes that the group

*included four women [who were] fully
aware of the fact that the death penalty
awaited anyone who accommodated or
otherwise helped saboteurs.*

One of those women
was Henny.

This was the "other work"
Mix had referred to
when they first met.
She felt
it was the right thing—
the just thing—to do,
to rid Denmark
of the foreign invaders
who had brought

war and violence to
their country.

She agreed with Jørgen
when he said,

> It was necessary to find the dividing line
> between Good and Evil.

As the HD2 group saw it,
the Nazis were
destroying their country,
their democracy,
their rights.
What the Nazis
were doing was Evil
and HD2 had to fight back.
It was war!

COMMAND CENTER

Mix, Henny, and other HD2
Resistance fighters met
at Mogens Staffeldt's bookstore.
It was their command center,
where they could
coordinate attacks
on German trains
and the factories
building Nazi weapons.

They received
some assistance from the Allies.
The British SOE
(Special Operations Executive)
supplied training
and information.
They flew in parachutists
armed with
bombs, explosives,
fuses, detonators.
Mix had told Henny the truth:
it was a dangerous business.

HENNY'S JOB

Among other things,
Henny conducted
scouting expeditions.
Before a planned
sabotage mission,
she would scope out the area
to see how many
Germans were around.

> *I usually walked with one of the boys and*
> *we were supposed to look very much in*
> *love, not caring about anything in the*
> *world except of the two of us and at the*
> *same time look around to see if there were*
> *any Germans. That is how I got into it*
> *and one thing led to another.*

Henny often walked with Mix,
and soon it wasn't
hard to pretend
to be in love.
For either of them.
Jørgen said,

they acted as [a] couple in connection with
sabotage, only to finally become [a couple]
for real.

ARM IN ARM

Working arm in arm,
side by side,
Henny and Mix
supported each other
as they embraced their cause.

No doubt about it—
Mix was an inspiring leader.
According to Jørgen,

> *He was much loved by his comrades,*
> *cadets and civilians alike. He was gifted,*
> *open and smiling, but also determined*
> *and resolute. He made no secret of the fact*
> *that he could be frightened; but he was*
> *courageous and never said no to joining in.*

While Mix assisted Jørgen
in his sabotage missions,
Henny did her part
by storing weapons,
arranging safe houses
for saboteurs,
and spying.

At least once, she used
her sister Bente's apartment
as a hideout.
It was on the top floor
of a building
next to her parents' house,
but Bente wasn't part of
the "illegal activities."
She just knew Henny was
involved with "something";
she didn't want to know what.
Bente would stay with a friend
when Henny needed the space.

Henny operated her hideout
right under the Nazis' noses.
There were Nazis
manning an office

on the ground floor.
Henny laughed,

What better cover could we get!

THE RISKS

If a Resistance fighter
was identified
by informants,
it was not only his or her life
that was in danger,
but the lives of everyone
in the entire organization.

Gerda III was one boat
that shepherded them
to safety in Sweden
before they could be arrested.

STILL SMUGGLING

Still *Gerda* sailed across the Sound,
smuggling Hope from port to port.
With fleeing Jews on safer ground,
still *Gerda* sailed across the Sound.
She imported arms and turned around,
to rescue Danes from German "court."
Still *Gerda* sailed across the Sound,
smuggling Hope from port to port.

SABOTAGE MISSIONS

In four months,
Holger Danske 2
succeeded in pulling off
twenty-five operations
that helped stop the Nazis from
manufacturing war material.

They blew up factories
that produced radio equipment
and sights for German bombers.

They blew up a steel mill
that made German weapons
and a shipyard that repaired
German submarines and warships.

Mix, the leader of the cadets,
was extra careful to avoid
unnecessary deaths—
of people or animals.
He remembered one mission:

> *When we went into action, we first had*
> *to move a horse-drawn cart that was*
> *standing nearby . . . for the horses' sake.*
> *When the explosion had happened, the*
> *police made arrangements to evacuate*
> *the nearest properties, as they feared new*
> *explosions. We then called the nearest*
> *police station and pointed out that it was*
> *unnecessary as no more would happen, and*
> *they seemed very happy to hear that.*

Other times, HD2
would warn the workers
ahead of an operation,
saying,

You have two minutes to get [out].

And get out
they did!

REPRIMAND

Navy leaders suspected
their cadets of sabotage—
a risky business for them all.
Mix was summoned,
reprimanded, and told to stop.
He requested time to think,
and time to confer
with the other cadets in HD2.
When he relayed
the navy's message,

> *[the cadets] agreed that they would not*
> *cease their sabotage activities under any*
> *circumstances. [However,] they offered to*
> *take their leave so that the navy would not*
> *be troubled on their account.*

When Mix reported back,
navy leaders had
changed their minds.

> They had found that Mix and his
> comrades could be a valuable source of
> information . . . and a compromise was
> reached. Provided they did not involve any
> more navy personnel in their work, Mix
> and the other cadets in HD2 were allowed
> to continue the sabotage. They were also
> to keep the staff up to date on everything
> important.

The navy was interested
in making contact
with the British SOE
and in developing a relationship
with the Danish Freedom Council.
Mix and his HD2 friends
were the link.

Meanwhile, they continued
their operations with each one
growing more daring
and more complicated.

Until one day,
HD2 made a mistake.

CATASTROPHE

Henny said,

Everything went wrong.

In early February 1944,
HD2 tried to
destroy two factories,
Hamag and Callesen,
just north of the German border
that were supplying equipment
for Nazi U-boats and warplanes.
The area was full of risk,
swarming with German troops
and sympathizers.
Several HD2 saboteurs
were captured by the Gestapo,
including Jørgen.
They knew they would be

interrogated, brutally.
Jørgen told his fellow prisoners,

> *Play for time, deny everything as long as*
> *possible.*

Word of their friends' arrest
rocketed throughout
the Resistance group.
Henny said,

> *I should have been dead scared if I had been*
> *taken by the Germans and I cannot tell . . .*
> *what I would have said if I was tortured.*
> *I don't know if I could have kept my mouth*
> *shut.*

GETAWAY

With part of the HD2 group
in prison,
everyone was in danger.
Henny, Mix, and the others
had to get away
before they were identified
and arrested.
Henny said,

> *It was too risky allowing [anyone]*
> *who knew too much . . . to stay [in*
> *Denmark] . . . It would be better for our*
> *friends who had been imprisoned by the*
> *Germans to know that the rest of the group*
> *had gotten away and were safe in Sweden.*
> *Then they could reveal names . . . if they*
> *were tortured by the Gestapo.*

Now after spiriting so many others
off to Sweden,
    it was Henny's turn to escape. . . .

PART XVII

The Tide Turns

GOING UNDERGROUND

Everyone in HD2
was ordered
to go into hiding
until they could be
evacuated to Sweden.
Henny said,

> *[It was] much against my will. We were all
> in deep despair.*
>
> *I was pretty mad when Mix came and told
> me. . . . I certainly didn't feel that I had
> accomplished anything yet, but Mix, who
> was constantly in talks with the leadership
> in the navy, had been ordered to see that
> everyone who [worked] with the cadets
> [was] sent off. It could . . . harm the navy if
> anything about its links with the sabotage
> was leaked.*
>
> *So . . . we all had to obey orders, and the
> whole group went underground.*

The group in prison
would get word
when everyone else
was safely evacuated.
Henny said,

> *In the prison, they had a very good*
> *knocking system from cell to cell. They*
> *had their own special language and they*
> *could tell each other if . . . a person had*
> *arrived safely in Sweden. When they were*
> *interrogated, they could use the name of*
> *that person, . . . which was very often a*
> *great help to the prisoners.*

TELLING HER PARENTS

Henny and the others
were given strict instructions.
They were not permitted to
go home, other than
one quick trip
to pack their things

and say goodbye to their families.
Now Henny had to admit
that she had been involved
in more than rescuing the Jews.

> *There was no way around it. I had to*
> *confess to my father and mother. I went up*
> *first and talked to Dad in the office. He*
> *was great, not a question, not a rebuke.*
> *[He] gave me the address of his Swedish*
> *colleague and good friend in Stockholm. . . .*
> *If I . . . needed help, I could always turn to*
> *him. That was nice to know.*

> *Mum was just as fantastic. . . . We cried a*
> *lot together when we said goodbye. In fact,*
> *she couldn't get me out the door fast enough*
> *and off to safety on the other side of the*
> *Sound.*

Henny rushed down the street.
Now days on the run
    for her own life
        had begun.

HIDEOUT

Henny couldn't go to *Gerda III*.
If the Nazis knew her name,
it would be among the first places
they looked.
She turned to Mix for help.

Mix . . . borrowed an apartment in
Nyboder, where I was to stay until I had
to leave (where he himself stayed at night,
I did not know). . . . He . . . provided a
"bodyguard" to look after me. . . . The
navy . . . was to get . . . routes for us, but
they were now somewhat slow. . . .

Luckily, Mix and I were in touch, and
every day we met at an agreed place and
time.

ONE LAST GOODBYE

Henny and Mix met
at Mogens Staffeldt's bookstore
on February 16 to get final details
for their evacuations and
for a last farewell.
Mogens, his brother, and Mix
were talking when
another employee
interrupted.

[He] said that there was someone in the
back room who wanted to talk to [them].
[Mogens's brother] asked us to wait a
moment and disappeared out the back.
Quite a long time passed and [he] didn't
come back. Mogens got a bit impatient
and went to get him. Neither of them came
back. [We] . . . waited a while. [The other
employee] quickly poked his head into the
shop and made some strange faces at us. We
realized that we were in trouble.

Henny and Mix
rushed out another door.

We never saw [Mogens's brother] again.
The Gestapo and their Danish henchmen
had come in through the back door, [and
taken both brothers]. We were deeply
shocked.

The Gestapo
took their prisoners
to headquarters
and would return
to search the bookstore
the next morning.
That night,
other Resistance fighters
emptied the shop's basement.
Good thing, too.
It had been stocked
with weapons and ammunition.

That same evening Mix and I said goodbye
to each other. I promised Mix that I would
stay indoors . . . with my bodyguard until I
was picked up for transport.

DIZZYING DAYS

Henny had to wait
for several days;
spinning between
tedium and terror.

> *It was not until late in the evening of*
> *20 February that I was picked up and*
> *driven to a villa . . . , which belonged to a*
> *Jewish family who had fled to Sweden.*

She did not know the man
who picked her up
and had to trust that all
would be well.
At the villa, she met
some of her HD2 friends
who would be escaping
with her.

They were scheduled to
be picked up by
a Danish police boat
arranged by the Danish navy,
but a stiff northeasterly gale
dashed their plan.

*The motorboat simply could not dock in
those conditions. We were driven back to the
villa . . . where we spent the night sleeping
on the floor, sofas . . . wherever else possible.*

*The next evening we were picked up and
driven to [another] house. . . . When it got
really dark, we were ordered one by one to
make our way down to the harbor where
the . . . boat now lay. Nearby there was a
German vessel with guards onboard.*

They sneaked past the guards,
boarded the boat,
and set off to sea.
But the danger wasn't over.

*We were . . . out into the Øresund [when]
we were observed and pursued by a
German patrol boat that fired some shots
at us.*

A moment later,
they realized
they were in trouble.
Their boat had been hit
and was taking on water.

PART XVIII

Seeking Safe Harbor

SINK OR SWIM?

Cold seawater
was rushing aboard.
The Danish policeman in charge
asked one of them to lie down
and work the wing pump.
Henny's friend Christian
volunteered.
He knew the danger:

> *If the flywheel of the engine got hold of the*
> *bottom water, the engine would soon break*
> *down due to water on the spark plugs and*
> *ignition magnet. I was very willing to take*
> *on the task of keeping the [boat going.]*

HOPE FLOATS

The German patrol boat
finally gave up the chase,
perhaps thinking
the Danes were doomed to sink.

For hours,
Henny's boat
plowed through the waves,
through the dark.
Soon the lights
on the Swedish coast
appeared,
winking and twinkling
with hope, with welcome.

In the early morning
of February 22,
Henny and her friends
made landfall in Råå, Sweden.
As the crow flies,
the distance was
about thirteen and a half kilometers
from Denmark
but it felt like a million kilometers:
a far shore from home,
but also a far cry from war.

Henny was wet,
and exhausted,
but full of relief
to stumble ashore in Sweden.

She was twenty-two years old,
far from family and friends,
exiled from her country,
but she was safe.
For now.
The Nazis couldn't reach her here.

SLEEP AND SWEETS

Henny and her friends
could relax for the first time
since the Nazi occupation.

> *We were taken to some "spa town," where*
> *we were allowed to crawl into some beds*
> *with lovely paper sheets that rattled and*
> *creaked if you moved in the slightest.*

Even refugee housing
with throwaway sheets
seemed like a luxury.

Later they were questioned
by the Swedish authorities,

medically examined,
given ration cards,
allowed to change money,
and sent to a boardinghouse
used as a transit camp
for refugees.
Henny's friend Christian
remembered,

> *It was a strange feeling to be in a country*
> *where there were no Germans walking*
> *the streets. In the evening there were lights*
> *on the streets, candles in every window,*
> *chocolate abounded in the shops. We gorged*
> *ourselves on chocolate . . . coffee, and tea.*

CONTINUING THE FIGHT

Where was Mix?
Henny wondered.
He had been evacuated
via a different route
and immediately
ordered to Stockholm.
Henny had to earn

a living in Sweden
so at first
she worked as a nanny.
She was sad to leave
her comrades behind.

Mix joined the Danish Brigade,
the Danish military in Sweden.
It was an elite force
of five to seven thousand,
including about 750 Jews—
young people who
were keen to join forces
with the Allies
and go back
to Denmark and fight.

Women weren't allowed
to join the brigade at first,
to Henny's
great annoyance.

*We were not very well received. The
men thought that girls were useless. We
had to show them [otherwise]. It took an
enormous effort.*

Eventually Henny
and other young women
did join and were provided
"an old hovel
three kilometers from camp."
They did office work
and cooked for the men
in the brigade,
even though
"she knew nothing
about cooking."
Henny said,

> *I'd rather be out in the field. It was more*
> *exciting than sitting in an office. . . .*
> *maybe it wasn't so feminine, but I didn't*
> *want my work to be particularly feminine.*

The months passed,
the seasons turned,
but by December
not much had changed.
Henny said,

> *In between, there were many tears. Almost*
> *every day someone got some terrible news*

from home about friends or acquaintances
who had died or been taken by the
Germans.

NEW YEAR'S EVE COUNTDOWN TO 1945

Exiled from family, there would be
no "jumping into the new year,"
no champagne, no sing-along,
no cod with mustard sauce,
no king's new year speech,
no fireworks.
Just more war,
far from
home.

A NEW YEAR, A STALEMATE

Henny spent
New Year's Eve
"with Mix and the boys"
at his training camp.
Henny wrote later,

> *Mix was determined that we should get
> married.*

They had talked it over for months,
but Henny wanted to wait
until the war was over,
until they could go home again.

> *I felt the future was so insecure and there
> were so many tasks for both of us to solve
> before marriage. . . . I did not like the idea
> of getting married without the knowledge
> of our parents—it just sounded terrible to me.*

Unfortunately,
Mix was not the waiting kind.

They rang in the new year,
but there was not much to celebrate.

When Mix and Henny parted,
both were very unhappy.

Mix was depressed and agitated,
on fire to fight,
to beat the Nazis.

For Henny, more anguish
was just days away.

A SHOCK

In early January,
Henny received a telegram
from friends in Mix's camp
with upsetting news.
It said,

Mix has left.

He had packed his weapon,
stolen a rowboat,
and rowed back across the Øresund,

back to Denmark.
Jørgen Kieler said,

> *The role of a passive observer was not for*
> *Mix.*

Mix wanted the war over
and he couldn't wait
any longer.

Henny couldn't believe it.
She made a call to his friends,
who were "just as confused"
as she was.
But they confirmed it was true.
Mix was gone.
Henny said,

> *I was full of admiration over the courage*
> *Mix had shown, . . . but I got a bit*
> *angry . . . a bit envious and deeply upset.*
> *I could not comprehend that he could go*
> *home without the rest of us, but he had*
> *apparently been more unhappy than I had*
> *realized. . . . An enormous feeling of guilt*
> *came over [me]. I was convinced that if*

I had sensed his intent I could, with one simple word ("YES"), have prevented him from leaving.

MORE BAD NEWS

Soon after,
Henny heard a Danish radio report
that her father had been arrested
by the Gestapo.
The Nazis kicked in the door
of their family home
at four a.m. on January 10.
Paul Sinding had certainly
been involved in his share of
"illegal work"—
working with
shipbuilding dockyards
to secretly build
six minesweepers
supposedly for
the lighthouse authorities,
suggesting "multiples of times

that we should send our ships
and boats to Sweden,"
among other things.

But no!
Contrary to what Henny heard,
it was not her father
who was arrested.
It was her eighteen-year-old brother, Carsten!

Henny didn't find out until
after the war
what had really happened.

> *[At four a.m.,] the Germans knocked and*
> *kicked the front door. . . . My mother who*
> *woke up with all the noise hurried to wake*
> *my dad. . . . He was very calm. "They*
> *can . . . wait till I am ready," he said. . . .*
> *There was one German and two [Danish*
> *Nazis]. They went through the whole*
> *house. They were very angry with my dad*
> *for [taking] such a long time to get ready.*
> *My parents did not think of Carsten. He*
> *was fast asleep, and it took them with*
> *total surprise when it turned out the*

Gestapo had come for him. . . . They found
Carsten's room and unfortunately . . . some
[Resistance newssheets]. He was pulled out
of bed and asked to get dressed and they
then left with him. My poor parents!

Paul Sinding
remembered,

The Gestapo . . . demonstrated their well-
known crude methods. . . . The worst
behavior was exhibited by [the lieutenant]
who was . . . brutal and snooty.

Carsten was arrested and imprisoned
in Vestre Prison and later sent
to the Frøslev Camp in Denmark,
often the last stop before
being shipped to a
concentration camp.

Carsten avoided deportation,
but it was not until after the war
that Carsten was released and
his family knew he had survived.

DISAPPEAR!

After the Nazi raid
and the capture of Carsten,
the Copenhagen harbor director
advised Henny's father
to disappear completely,
and promised to do the same.
Henny's father said,

> *Both my wife and I went into hiding from*
> *February and lived separately with some*
> *friends.*

There was good cause for concern.
When he was not at home,
someone tried to break into his house.
They had murder in mind.
Paul Sinding said,

> *Someone had seen a Gestapo car in front of*
> *my door, people with machine guns stood*
> *ready on each side, while a third man tried*
> *to pick the lock.*

Thankfully, they were unsuccessful.
But eight days later

Paul's colleague,
the harbor director,
was murdered.
He had not gone into hiding
as he had promised.

WAITING FOR WORD

In Sweden,
Henny worried and waited
for any news of
her loved ones.
Thankfully,
over the next two months,
she started
to receive mail
from Mix
that was smuggled
across the Øresund by
an illegal courier service.

Mix wrote
of his continuing fight
against the Nazis.

Being here is a little like driving along a cliff. I have thought several times that my luck was running out but was fortunate at the last minute. . . . Here we are expecting the end [of the war] very soon and our optimism is great.

One of HD2's successes
at the time
was blowing up the
Burmeister & Wain
shipbuilding yard
that was furnishing ships
to the Germans.
Jørgen called it HD2's
"greatest achievement"
and gave Mix "particular credit"
for that mission's success.

A TERRIBLE DISAPPOINTMENT

One letter
written by Mix
on February 23, 1945,
reached Henny
on March 4.
It had bad news.

Mix and his team had tried
to blow up a coal ship
at the entrance to the
Copenhagen harbor.

It would have been a triumph—
stopping Nazi ships from entering
and preventing coal
from reaching Germany.

Mix only told Henny,

> *My team had a terrible disappointment.*
> *A job did not succeed. . . . How I long for*
> *you. . . . We had our time and it will come*
> *again when this is over.*

WHAT HENNY DIDN'T KNOW

In the time that the letter
was bundled on a boat to Sweden,
Mix was betrayed by an informant.

In the time that the letter
traveled the stormy sea,
the Gestapo stormed Mix's apartment
and he was captured.

In the time that the letter
arrived on Sweden's shore,
Mix and others on his team
were being led
to a Nazi firing squad.

In the time that the letter
was headed out
for delivery to Henny,
Mix tried to escape.

ONE DAY BEFORE

One day before
Henny opened
the letter . . .

One day before
she read
the words he had written,

> *We had our time and it will come again*
> *when this is over . . .*

One day before
she thought of
their future together . . .

Mix was shot.

Henny's "dynamic navy cadet" died,
killed by the Nazis
as he tried to escape
on March 3, 1945.

He was twenty-one years old.

IF ONLY

If only
Mix had known
that in two months' time,
German troops in Denmark,
Holland, and Norway
would surrender.

If only
Mix had known
that Denmark would survive the war,
that 7,742 Jews would survive the war,
that Henny and her family would survive the war.

If only
Mix had known
his death would leave Henny devastated,
      alone in limbo.

If only he had waited.
If only.

IT'S OVER

Two months later,
on May 4, 1945,
Henny remembered
her group being
called over to
an officer's tent.

> *And then we heard the BBC, this da–da–*
> *da–dum, da–da–da–dum, and a Danish*
> *speaker from England.*

Interrupting the news report,
he read a telegram saying,

> *All German forces in Northwest Germany,*
> *Holland, and Denmark have surrendered.*
> *This surrender becomes effective at 8 o'clock*
> *tomorrow morning.*

Dumbfounded,
the Danish Brigade
had a surprising response.
They were furious!

They hadn't had a chance
to fight the Nazis.
Some cried,
some started shooting,
some threw hand grenades.

Henny said,

> *It may sound strange, but. . . . I broke
> down sobbing. . . . Everyone was so
> disappointed. They had been working on
> coming home and throwing the Germans
> out for so many months.*
>
> *The thought that we didn't get to . . . was
> just horrible. Indeed, we thought it had all
> been in vain.*

Once everyone quieted down,
orders came through to
pack up camp.

Henny and the others
gathered their things
and climbed into vehicles
for the drive south.

They were headed
to a port where they would
board a boat
back to Denmark.
All along the way,
celebration lit up
the night streets.
Henny said,

> *And everywhere, we drove through Sweden,*
> *the Swedes were in the streets. This was*
> *in the middle of the night, but even so, the*
> *Swedes were in the streets with Danish flags*
> *and Swedish flags and waving.*

The Danes were going home.

PART XIX

Homeward Bound

PASSAGE

Henny and the others
drove through the night
and near six a.m.
the next morning,
Henny and her friends
boarded the ferry
named *Holger Danske*
that would bear them
back home.
For all the young Resistance fighters,
going west across the Øresund
with the sun rising on their backs,
the circle would soon be complete.
The Germans were gone
and Denmark was *their* country once again.
Henny didn't remember the trip at all.
Once onboard,
she fell into a deep sleep.

> *Suddenly I felt someone pushing me and*
> *[saying] "Wake up." . . . I was lying on one*
> *of the stoves, which was still warm. And*
> *I had . . . slept all the way over. I was so*
> *tired. We were so tired, all of us.*

ECHO OF THE BARD

When the ferry landed,
Danes everywhere
were celebrating the news.
Henny said,

> *There were many, many people with flags*
> *and shouting and some were crying. And it*
> *was a very great welcome we got.*

They came ashore in Helsingør,
in northern Denmark,
the setting of Shakespeare's
famous play *Hamlet*
that had told of something
"rotten in the state of Denmark."
For Henny, the "something rotten"
had been swept away.
They had their country back.
The bard's "words, words, words"—
"to thine own self be true"—
echoed all that had happened
to Henny and the Danes.

ELEGY

Mix's body was found
north of Copenhagen.
Henny's love was just one
of 196 Resistance fighters
uncovered in a field where the Nazis
had executed them.

In August 1945,
Mix and others
who had died
received their due.
Each was given
a hero's funeral
in a procession
led by King Christian X?

The caskets,
showered with flowers,
were solemnly paraded
through Copenhagen.
Flags flew at half-mast
while bells tolled
and grateful Danes lined
the streets to pay

their last respects.
Mix was buried
in the hallowed ground
of Ryvangen Memorial Park,
a site ultimately commemorating
more than three hundred and eighty
Danish freedom fighters
who had given their lives
to fight for what was right.

One of those who came
to mourn that day,
and for many days to come,
was Henny.

BEING HUMAN

Henny knew the Danes
had done the right thing—
the only human thing—
in fighting the Nazis,
in standing up for their people.
In the words of author Elie Wiesel,

those who had fought the Nazis
"climbed to the summit
of humanity
by simply remaining human."

And yet, like the Little Mermaid,
Henny discovered
that being human can be painful
and not without its price.

STILL STANDING

Like Drogden Lighthouse,
Henny was battered by the war,
shell-shocked, but still standing.
Like the lighthouse,
she survived
by continuing
to be of service.

As part of the
Danish Brigade,
Henny helped clear mines

planted by the Nazis.
She joined the
Danish Red Cross
in Holland
to help children
freed from Nazi
concentration camps
recover from their ordeal.

Like Drogden Lighthouse,
Henny survived
by radiating light
for those in need,
showing them
        the way home.

Just as light on the water
bends, refracts,
and reflects back,
hope in the eyes of people
she helped—
people who had suffered so much—
found its way back to Henny.

She took it to heart.
Harboring hope

helped Henny
get her bearings,
find a deep channel
through her grief,
and start again.

SAILING ON

Henny went back to her first love—
the ever-constant sea.
Sailing the Øresund,
she consoled herself
on the gently rocking waves.
It took time, a long time,
but one day fresh breezes
billowed her sails.
She went back to racing
her Dragon sloop,
buoyant with the fearlessness
she had as a child.

In 1947, she married her
childhood sailing friend

Erling Sundø,
who had also been
in the Resistance,
been evacuated to Sweden,
and been part of
the Danish Brigade.
Together they
raised two daughters
and got on with living
a good life.

But the war
and her days
in the Danish Resistance
shaped her.
Henny said,

> *I don't think a day goes by when I don't*
> *think about those . . . months. I lost a lot of*
> *buddies [whom] I think about every day.*
> *Those of us who are still alive stick together*
> *and enjoy each other very much.*

GRATITUDE

Henny never expected
thanks for her efforts.
After the war, people
didn't talk about
what had happened.
Henny said that
everyone was too busy
moving on.

*Myself included. . . . We didn't ask
questions [or try] to find the people
who helped [us]. So you never had the
opportunity really to thank [them]. . . .
You would never say to a person, "What
did you do during the war?" You wouldn't
dream of doing that. And you wouldn't
dream of telling what you had been doing
yourself. It was just taboo.*

*I have never expected a thank-you from
the people I helped escape, and I have never
thought to seek any of the people who helped
me. It was just something you did.*

It wasn't until a press event
fifty years after the escape of the Jews
that Henny met Gerd Lilienfeldt—
the boy who had been captured
in the Gilleleje Church—
and he was able to thank her.

Neither remembered the other;
after all, it had been
the dead of night
when she had guided him
to the warehouse and
onto *Gerda III.*
He was just one
of many desperate faces
in the dark.

There were many faces
she hadn't known
or hadn't recognized.

FULL CIRCLE

After the war,
Henny received
a large package at the door—
rectangular,
big enough
that she had to grasp it
with two hands.
It was addressed to her.
Who was it from?
What was inside?

Henny unwrapped it to find
a shock.
Inside was a gift,
a memento
that meant everything to her—
  childhood,
  family,
  war,
  danger,
  love,
  courage,
  care,
  gratitude.

A reminder of all
that had happened.
All that Henny,
her family and friends,
and her country
        had lived through.

There in the wrapping
was the picture
her father had painted,
the one that had hung over her bed,
of a lighthouse crewman
tending a red-and-white buoy
halfway between Denmark
and Sweden.

It was the painting her father
had given to his Jewish friend,
the merchant who wouldn't give it back.

This man had been
another unrecognized face
she had led down the dark streets,
had hidden in the warehouse,
had told to run to *Gerda III.*
There was a small note

attached to the painting,
with one sentence that
spoke volumes,
encapsulating all
Henny had done.

It read simply,
"Thank you for my life."

Ship's Log

MORE ABOUT HENNY, *GERDA III*, AND THE ESCAPE OF THE DANISH JEWS

Henny and the crew of *Gerda III* successfully aided more than three hundred Jews, perhaps more than any other boat. After the Jews were safely ashore in Sweden, *Gerda III* evacuated an additional six hundred to seven hundred people, including Danish Resistance fighters and downed Allied airmen and parachutists.

> *About 99 percent of the Jews in Denmark survived while 98 percent of Poland's three million Jews perished.*
> —HERBERT PUNDIK

Refugee Records

An estimated one thousand Danes (including Jews) had taken refuge in Sweden up until October 1, 1943. After the roundup, the Swedish navy and police force kept approximate records of how many refugees arrived in Sweden each day in October 1943. What started out as 100 or so people on October 1 grew to 1,100 on October 8 and 1,400 on October 9, the peak days for evacuations. By the end of October, 90 percent of the Jews were safely across. Spouses and small children continued to make the journey into November and December. Recent figures show that 7,742 Jews fled to Sweden because of the German action. By the end of the war eighteen months later, in May 1945, there were about 18,000 Danish refugees in Sweden: Jews plus freedom fighters, politicians, police, military, and so on.

Jewish Refugees in Sweden at the End of the War in May, 1945

According to Danish historian Therkel Straede, there were:

- 7,906 Danish-Jewish refugees in Sweden, including 686 non-Jewish spouses.
- 1,364 refugee children under fifteen years of age, including babies born in Sweden. More than 1,000

were under the age of ten.

- 1,376 Jews from Denmark were stateless exiles; 348 chose to stay in Sweden after the war.
- 435 were agricultural students (Halutzim) and Aliyah children.

The Danish Jewish Museum created a website and database that can be searched to find people who fled Denmark for Sweden from October 1943 to June 1945. According to Professor Straede at the University of Southern Denmark, "Many reports are unspecific as to the details of the travel, mostly because the Jews had promised the helpers not to mention anything that might help identifying them or their vessels." So the database is not a complete list, but it includes some six thousand people. Visit safe-haven.dk.

HOMECOMING

Some refugees returned to Denmark to find that their apartments had been rented to others due to a housing shortage and were forced to find temporary living quarters elsewhere. But many, like Aron Engelhardt, came home to find their apartments were still there, just as they had left them, or even better.

Many neighbors cared for the Jewish refugees' homes during the war, cleaning and painting them, even taking care of their pets. They were welcomed home with open arms.

Many people had had to leave their businesses without warning, but civil servants got their jobs back and some even received a full salary during their absence.

The synagogue in Copenhagen reopened on June 22, 1945, and Jews worked to return to the lives they had before the occupation.

The White Buses

Jews who had been captured and sent to Theresienstadt (in what is now the Czech Republic) were starved and brutally treated, but they were not sent on to places like Auschwitz, where Jews were killed. Danes never forgot them. They sent food, medicine, and inspectors, and ultimately, a joint Danish-Norwegian-Swedish operation saved the prisoners. On April 15, 1945, twenty-three white buses from the Red Cross, accompanied by Danish doctors and nurses, made the dangerous trip to pick up 423 Scandinavian Jews, drive them to northern Germany, and ferry them to safety in Sweden.

The White Buses also saved Jørgen Kieler and Erling Sundø's brother Erik, who had been imprisoned in the concentration camp Porta Westphalica in Hamburg, Germany.

Punishment for Informants

The Danish Freedom Council warned that "every Dane who [helps] the Germans . . . is a traitor and will be punished as such when Germany is defeated." Sure enough, "stikkers" (informants) or collaborators were dealt with: "15,000 were arrested; 13,521 found guilty. Forty-six [death sentences] were carried out."

Righteous Among the Nations

After World War II, Yad Vashem (the World Holocaust Remembrance Center in Israel) honored non-Jews who helped Jews escape during the war as "Righteous Among the Nations." While countries like the Netherlands have more than five thousand people so honored, there are only twenty-two named in Denmark. Why so few? In the 1960s, the Danish Resistance decided they wanted to be honored as a group, not as individuals. Modern historians point out that the many fishing captains who received a fee to ferry the Jews to Sweden would be ineligible for this honor. Others point to a laissez-faire attitude by many Germans who did not agree with the persecution and looked the other way. In hindsight, some historians discount the danger to the Jews and the Danes who helped them. They seem to ignore the Jews who were shipped off to Theresienstadt concentration camp, those who drowned in the Øresund, those who were captured and tortured. The Danish people believed they were in danger . . . and helped anyway. Many like Henny and *Gerda III* operated without payment and in fear for their lives. And yet they required no acknowledgment. As Henny said, "I have never expected a thank-you from the people I helped escape. . . . It was just something you did." In a 1997 letter, Henny wrote, "I am rather embarrassed that you praise the Danish people so highly. It seems as if the American people look upon the Danes as heroes. We were not heroes. I am convinced that the American people would have done the same."

The reality of what Denmark did . . . is more powerful than myth. And as future generations recall the brutality and the evil, as they must . . . they will also recall the strong, steady light of decency— undimmed by the darkness surrounding it—that sparkled from this precious . . . Denmark.
—Meyer Lieman at a ceremony honoring Righteous Gentiles in Denmark, 1997

WHAT HAPPENED TO
GERDA III?

After the war, *Gerda III* continued her daily duties for forty-one years. In 1989, the Danish parliament donated the *Gerda III* (restored to her wartime appearance) to the Museum of Jewish Heritage in New York City. They enlisted the Mystic Seaport Museum in Connecticut to care for the boat and preserve it. About six hundred boats spirited the Danish Jews off to Sweden; *Gerda III* is one of three now afloat and on display. Look for a new exhibit about *Gerda III* and the Danish Resistance at the Museum of Jewish Heritage—A Living Memorial to the Holocaust, in New York City. For more information, visit mjhnyc.org.

Gerda III *now docked in Connecticut* (Mystic Seaport Museum, Joe Michael)

PHOTOGRAPHS

Photographs are courtesy of the Sundø family unless otherwise noted.

Henny's sister, Bente (front left), Henny with bag beside her, their mom (left), and aunt (right), and other friends

Henny with her accordion (ca. 1937–38)

The four-room house where Henny was born, part of a row house in the navy barracks called Nyboder
(Susan Hood)

View of Henny's teenage home

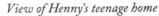

Henny as a teenager (front right)

*Henny's father, Naval Commander
Paul Sinding, in his full dress uniform*

Paul Sinding painting in his attic studio

Henny's mother, Elna ("Chika") Sinding

Henny sailing

Copenhagen's bronze statue of the Little Mermaid, based on the fairy tale by Hans Christian Andersen, shows her becoming human when her fishtail turns into legs. (Susan Hood)

Oprop leaflets dropped by German planes on the day of the invasion (The Museum of Danish Resistance)

Oprop leaflet, telling Danes to remain calm (The Museum of Danish Resistance)

Nazis in the streets
(THE MUSEUM OF DANISH RESISTANCE)

*King Christian X on his daily horseback ride th[...]
Copenhagen* (THE MUSEUM OF DANISH RESISTAN[...]

*"The Bloodhound of
Paris" Nazi Werner Best*
(THE MUSEUM OF DANISH
RESISTANCE)

*Georg Duckwitz, the
German who tipped off
Danes about the coming
Nazi roundup*
(THE MUSEUM OF DANISH
RESISTANCE)

Scuttling of the fleet, August 1943. The Danish navy sank their own ships to prevent the Germans from using them. (The Museum of Danish Resistance)

Danish protesters overturned German cars in Odense, 1943
(The Museum of Danish Resistance)

Gerda III—forty-foot workboat for the Danish Lighthouse and Buoy Service, which made daily trips to supply the Drogden Lighthouse in the middle of the Øresund strait between Denmark and Sweden. (HISTORICAL ARCHIVES, DRAGØR)

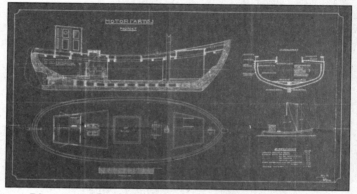

Blueprint of Gerda III (COURTESY OF THE MUSEUM OF JEWISH HERITAGE—A LIVING MEMORIAL TO THE HOLOCAUST)

Hans Just's warehouse, where Henny hid the Jewish families waiting for escape on Gerda III (HISTORICAL ARCHIVES, DRAGØR)

The fish hold in Gerda III *where ten to fifteen Jewish men, women, and children hid each night.*
(Susan Hood)

Gerda III *Captain Ejnar Tønnesen*
(Courtesy of his granddaughter
Kirsten Tønnesen)

Portrait of Gerda III, *painted by Captain Ejnar Tønnesen* (Courtesy of Jens Wagner
and Kirsten Tønnesen)

Dragør fishing village, home of the Gerda III *crew and the Drogden Lighthouse keepers*
(Susan Hood)

Drogden Lighthouse, 2022
(SUSAN HOOD)

Resistance fighter Jørgen Kieler
(THE MUSEUM OF DANISH RESISTANCE)

Resistance fighter and bookstore owner Mogens Staffeldt (THE MUSEUM OF DANISH RESISTANCE)

A modern photo of boats on the Danish shore showing Sweden across the Øresund, 2022 (SUSAN HOOD)

Gilleleje Church, on the coast in northern Denmark (Susan Hood)

Gilleleje Church attic, where Jews were hidden (Susan Hood)

Gestapo chief Hans Juhl, who captured the Jews hidden in Gilleleje Church, including Gerd Lilienfeldt

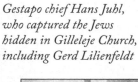

A young Gerd Lilienfeldt with his family, just before he left Germany for Denmark (Courtesy of Gerd's son, Sigurd Lilienfeldt)

Henny and Mix in the Danish Brigade, 1944

Henny in the Danish Brigade in Sweden, 1944

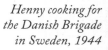

Henny cooking for the Danish Brigade in Sweden, 1944

Where Mix was shot by the Germans, after he returned to Denmark
(SUSAN HOOD)

Today, a plaque still commemorates the place where Mix died in 1945
(SUSAN HOOD)

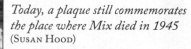

Mix's grave at Ryvangen Memorial Park, north of Copenhagen (FLEMMING SUNDØ)

←

→

Annual May 4 ceremony at Ryvangen Memorial Park, commemorating Resistance fighters who died for their country (SUSAN HOOD)

Flowers laid in honor of Holger Danske Resistance fighters, 2022 (SUSAN HOOD)

Henny sailing after the war

Henny with her future husband, Erling Sundø, 1946

Painting by Paul Sinding, returned to Henny after the war with a note that read, "Thank you for my life."

Henny (ca. 1958)

POETRY NOTES

Most of this book is written in *free verse*, which has no set meter or rhyme scheme. However, it uses poetic techniques, such as alliteration, anaphora, assonance, onomatopoeia, refrains, rhythm, and so on. Other poetic forms used in this book are as follows:

"Lifeboat" (p. 51) is an *ode*, which means it celebrates a person, animal, object, or idea. It often has no formal structure and may or may not rhyme.

"*Gerda III*'s Destination: Drogden Light" (p. 54) is a *concrete* or *shape poem*, where words are arranged to form a picture of the subject of the poem. It can rhyme or not.

"The Scales of Injustice" (pp. 72–73) is also a *shape poem*.

"Graffiti Protests" (p. 119) is a *cinquain*, a form of poetry composed of five lines with a pattern of two, four, six, eight, and two syllables.

"Rumors Whirling" (p. 171) is a *shape poem*.

"H for Helping Hands" (p. 185) is an *ABC poem*, which uses words with initial letters from *A* to *Z*.

"Enough!" (p. 214) is a *sensory poem*. It describes a scene, object, or idea with words that appeal to the five senses. It tells how something smells, tastes, feels, looks, and sounds.

"So Many Lives, So Many Stories" (p. 246) is a *list poem*, a list or inventory of items, people, places, or ideas that includes repetition and may or may not rhyme. The last line or so makes a point about items in the list.

"Still Smuggling" (p. 297) is a *triolet*, an eight-line poem in which line one repeats as lines four and seven and line two repeats as line eight. The rhyme scheme is ABaAabAB; the capital letters show lines that repeat.

"New Year's Eve Countdown to 1945" (p. 322) is a *nonet*, a poem of nine lines. The first line has nine syllables, the second eight, and so on, until the last line ends with one syllable.

"Elegy" (p. 342) is named for its form. An *elegy* is a poem used to praise or mourn the dead, so it often has a sad or somber tone. Elegies follow no set pattern.

SOURCES

WEBSITES

Henny Sinding, *Gerda III*, and the Danish Resistance
Henny Sinding Sundø: "The 22-Year-Old Woman Behind the
    Rescue of Over 300 Danish Jews"
mjhnyc.org/the-22-year-old-woman-behind-the-rescue-of-over
    -300-danish-jews
Gerda III: Danish Lighthouse Tender
www.mysticseaport.org/explore/vessels/gerda-iii-danish-lighthouse
    -tender
Mystic Seaport Museum for Educators: The *Gerda III*
https://educators.mysticseaport.org/artifacts/gerda_iii

October 23: The Rescue of the Danish Jews from Annihilation
natmus.dk/fileadmin/user_upload/Editor/natmus/frihedsmuseet
    /October_1943_The_Rescue_of_the_Danish_Jews_from
    _Annihilation.pdf

**Oral histories, maps, photographs, and other artifacts
of Denmark during World War II, from the United States
Holocaust Memorial Museum**
encyclopedia.ushmm.org/tags/en/tag/denmark

Danish Rescue Groups
www.holocaustrescue.org/danish-organizations

A Teacher's Guide to the Holocaust
fcit.usf.edu/HOLOCAUST/resource/Website.htm#rescuers

Yad Vashem
The rescue of the Jews of Denmark by the Danish people:
www.yadvashem.org/odot_pdf/Microsoft%20Word%20-%206756.pdf

About the Righteous Among the Nations
www.yadvashem.org/righteous.html
www.yadvashem.org/righteous/about-the-righteous.html

Righteous Database:
righteous.yadvashem.org/?searchType=all&language=en

Modern Historians' Viewpoints
A New Perspective on the Rescue of the Danish Jews. Recording from the Museum of Jewish Heritage—A Living Memorial to the Holocaust: mjhnyc.org/blog/a-new-perspective-on-the -rescue-of-denmarks-jews
"Copenhagen: Bright Hope and Deep Gloom—A New Perspective of the 1943 Rescue Operation in Denmark," by Sofie Lene Bak: www.humanityinaction.org/knowledge_detail/copenhagen -bright-hope-and-deep-gloom-a-new-view-of-the-1943-rescue -operation-in-denmark/

AUTHOR INTERVIEWS
Henny's daughter Lillan Sundø and nephew Flemming Sundø, 2020, 2021, 2022
Gerd Lilienfeldt's son Sigurd Lilienfeldt, 2022
Danish naval expert Søren Nørby, 2021
Dr. Therkel Straede, Professor of Contemporary History, University of Southern Denmark, 2021

ARCHIVES
Letters and photographs courtesy of Lillan and Flemming Sundø and the Dragør Local Archives

FIRST-PERSON ACCOUNTS

Oral History with Henny Sundø
    United States Holocaust Memorial Museum
    collections.ushmm.org/search/catalog/irn513388
Sundø, Henny Sinding. *Henny's Story: A Woman in the Resistance.*
    Edited by Winnie Wickman Jørgensen and Gunnar J. Blaschke.
    Translated by Malene Sølvdahl Clementsen. Forsvarets
    Oplysnings-og Velfaerdstjeneste, 1995.
Oral History with Jørgen Kieler
    United States Holocaust Memorial Museum
    collections.ushmm.org/search/catalog/irn513384
Oral History with Ebba Lund
    United States Holocaust Memorial Museum.
    collections.ushmm.org/search/catalog/irn513389
Oral History with Mogens Staffeldt
    United States Holocaust Memorial Museum
    collections.ushmm.org/search/catalog/irn513326
Interview with Aron Engelhardt. Translated by Malene Sølvdahl
    Clementsen. Excerpt from history essay from University of
    Roskilde, 1993.

BOOKS AND MEMOIRS

Leo Goldberger

"Personal Narrative." *The Rescue of the Danish Jews: Moral Courage
    under Stress.* Leo Goldberger, editor. New York: New York
    University Press, 1987. pp. 157–167.

Jørgen Kieler

"Personal Narrative." *The Rescue of the Danish Jews: Moral Courage
    under Stress.* Leo Goldberger, editor. New York: New York
    University Press, 1987. pp. 141–155.
Kieler, Jørgen. *The Story of a Resistance Group.* Translated by Ann
    Kravitz. self-pub., Copenhagen, Denmark, 1982.
Kieler, Jørgen, and Eric Dickens. *Resistance Fighter: A Personal
    History of the Danish Resistance Movement 1940–1945.* Jerusalem,

Israel: Gefen Books, 2010.

Kieler, Jørgen. *Why Did You Do It? Volume 1: Personal Accounts from the Occupation in a Historical Perspective*. Copenhagen, Gyldendal, 2001.

Herbert Pundik

In Denmark It Could Not Happen: The Flight of the Jews to Sweden in 1943. Jerusalem, Israel: Gefen Books, 1998.

"Personal Narrative." *The Rescue of the Danish Jews: Moral Courage under Stress*. Leo Goldberger, editor. New York: New York University Press, 1987. pp. 77–97.

Paul Sinding

Memoirs of Paul Sinding, director of the Danish Lighthouse and Buoy Service. Arkiv.dk—PDF Viewer.
Accessed January 08, 2022. arkiv.dk/pdfviewer /viewpdf?originalId=83ae9853956c4afd97d9c49a9002eb6a.

Peter H. Tveskov

Conquered, Not Defeated: Growing Up in Denmark During the German Occupation of World War II. Central Point, Oregon: Hellgate Press, 2003.

BIBLIOGRAPHY

Birkelund, Peter. "Sabotør i Holger Danske" ["Saboteur in Holger Danske"]. Translated by Malene Sølvdahl Clementsen. Copenhagen: Lindhardt og Ringhof, 2015.

Byers, Ann. *Rescuing the Danish Jews: A Heroic Story from the Holocaust (The Holocaust Through Primary Sources)*. Berkeley Heights, NJ: Enslow, 2012.

Flender, Harold. *Rescue in Denmark*. New York: Simon and Schuster, 1963.

Goldberger, Leo, editor. *The Rescue of the Danish Jews: Moral Courage under Stress*. New York: New York University Press, 1987.

Halter, Marek. *Stories of Deliverance: Speaking with Men and Women Who Rescued Jews from the Holocaust*. Translated by Michael Bernard. La Salle, IL: Open Court Publishing, 1998.

Hoose, Phillip. *The Boys Who Challenged Hitler: Knud Pedersen and the Churchill Club*. New York: Farrar Straus Giroux, 2015.

Hopkinson, Deborah. *Courage & Defiance: Spies, Saboteurs, and Survivors in World War II Denmark*. New York: Scholastic, 2016.

Lampe, David. *Hitler's Savage Canary: A History of the Danish Resistance in World War II*. New York: Arcade Publishing, 2014.

Levine, Ellen. *Darkness over Denmark: The Danish Resistance and the Rescue of the Jews*. New York: Holiday House, 2000.

Lidegaard, Bo. *Countrymen: The Untold Story of How Denmark's Jews Escaped the Nazis, the Courage of Their Fellow Danes—and of the Extraordinary Role of the SS*. New York: Knopf, 2013.

Lowry, Lois. *Number the Stars*. Reissue edition. New York: Clarion, 2011.

Veisz, Howard. *Henny's Boat: The Maritime Rescue Operation that Saved Denmark's Jews and Sparked a Nationwide Revolt Against the Nazis*. 2022.

Werner, Emmy E. *A Conspiracy of Decency: The Rescue of the Danish Jews During World War II*. Boulder, CO: Westview Press, 2002.

Yahil, Leni. *The Rescue of the Danish Jewry: Test of a Democracy*. Philadelphia: Jewish Publication Society of America, 1969.

QUOTE SOURCES

Author's note: Danish sources translated by Malene Sølvdahl Clementsen and Sarah Vestergaard Andersen.

Page vii: *"In those times..."* Elie Wiesel, foreword to *The Courage to Care: Rescuers of Jews During the Holocaust.* Carol Rittner and Sondra Myers, eds. New York: New York University Press, 1986: xi.

Page vii: *"There is always light..."* Peter Armenti. "'For There Is Always Light': Amanda Gorman's Inaugural Poem 'The Hill We Climb' Delivers Message of Unity." From the Catbird Seat: Poetry & Literature at the Library of Congress (blog), January 22, 2021. blogs.loc.gov/catbird/2021/01/for-there-is-always-light-amanda-gormans-inaugural -poem-the-hill-we-climb-delivers-message-of-unity/

Page vii: *"Denmark caused us more difficulties..."* Therkel Straede. *October 1943: The Rescue of the Danish Jews from Annihilation.* H. Rovsing Olsen, ed. Copenhagen: Royal Danish Ministry of Foreign Affairs and the Museum of Danish Resistance 1940–1945, 1993: 25.

Page vii: *"Whoever saves one life..."* Paraphrased from the Talmud in Gideon Fraser, "To Save the World Entire." United States Holocaust Memorial Museum, November 1, 2013. ushmm.org/remember/holocaust-reflections-testimonies/echoes-of-memory/to-save-the -world-entire

Page 7: *"taken, simply"* Oral History with Henny Sundø.

Page 25: *"couldn't be bothered with him, just a baby"*; *"boring because she always did what she was told"*; *"Bente was a rather quiet girl..."* Author interview with Lillan and Flemming Sundø.

Page 29: *"Your family name...";* *"good inner moral compass";"One does not boast..."* Author interview with Lillan and Flemming Sundø.

Page 32: *"destined to become ladies of pleasure..."* Author interview with Lillan and Flemming Sundø.

Page 33: *"strongest girl in the world"* Astrid Lindgren. *Pippi Longstocking.* New York: Puffin, 2005.

Page 34: *"had her own little faith"*; *"something else, something bigger"*; *"If somebody comes asking you for help..."* Author interview with Lillan and Flemming Sundø.

Page 35: *"In our family, we do not gossip!"* Author interview with Lillan and Flemming Sundø.

Page 36: *"Uncle Bob"* Author interview with Lillan and Flemming Sundø.

Page 37: *"force of nature"* Author interview with Lillan and Flemming Sundø.

Page 38: *"Look after your teeth!"*; *"Learn languages!"* Author interview with Lillan and Flemming Sundø.

Page 39: *"ever curious and daring child"* Author interview with Lillan and Flemming Sundø.

Page 42: *"Germany has invaded Poland..."* 4TheRecord. "BBC News—Lionel Marson Reports on Invasion of Poland—September 1, 1939." YouTube, September 6, 2016. youtube.com /watch?v=ktn_P5z5MK4

Page 43: *"This country is at war with Germany...."* "BBC News—Lionel Marson Reports on Invasion of Poland—September 1, 1939"; "Prime Minister Chamberlain Declares War." BBC News, September 1, 1999. news.bbc.co.uk/1/hi/special_report/1999/08/99 /world_war_ii/430071.stm

Page 43: *"to maintain peace"* "Judgement: The Invasion of Denmark and Norway." Avalon Project, Yale Law School. Lillian Goldman Law Library. avalon.law.yale.edu/imt/ juddenma.asp

Page 44: *"under all circumstances"* "Judgement: The Invasion of Denmark and Norway." Avalon Project, Yale Law School. Lillian Goldman Law Library. avalon.law.yale.edu /imt/juddenma.asp

Page 44: *"Her father kept things to himself...."* Author interview with Lillan and Flemming Sundø.

Page 48: *"everything... to do with the sea"* Oral History with Henny Sundø.

Page 56: *"You could get seasickness..."* Kieler, *The Story of a Resistance Group.*

Page 60: *"The Danes were clearly surprised..."* Author interview with Lillan and Flemming Sundø.

Page 64: *"From my window . . ."* Goldberger, 158.

Page 65: *"I was awakened . . ."* Goldberger, 141.

Page 68: *"I considered continued fighting pointless . . ."* Lidegaard, 17.

Page 75: *"We are all his bodyguards."* Werner, 14.

Page 76: *"Silk and later nylon stockings . . ."* Tveskov, 37.

Page 77: *"Heating fuel became so scarce . . ."* Levine, 15.

Page 77: *"I will survive. . . ."* Author interview with Flemming Sundø.

Page 78: *"armed guests . . ."* Goldberger, 158.

Page 79: *"a model protectorate"* Lampe, 1.

Page 79: *"our flagship"* Pundik, *In Denmark It Could Not Happen*, loc. 1471, Kindle.

Page 79: *"a state of paralysis"* Oral History with Jørgen Kieler.

Page 79: *"the sadistic murderer's canary"* Lampe, 1.

Page 81: *"I [receive] my orders from my own ministry . . ."* Memoirs of Paul Sinding.

Page 81: *"I would not take part . . ."* Memoirs of Paul Sinding.

Page 82: *"den kolde skulder"* Werner, 11.

Page 82: *"sophisticated form of civil disobedience"* Author interview with Flemming Sundø.

Page 83: *"I do not see you"* Author interview with Flemming Sundø.

Page 83: *"they would not be met . . ."* Author interview with Flemming Sundø.

Page 83: *"inferior race"* "Nazi Racism." Holocaust Encyclopedia. United States Holocaust Memorial Museum. encyclopedia.ushmm.org/content/en/article/nazi-racism

Page 83: *"vermin"* "The Final Solution, Chapter IV." Library of Social Science newsletter. libraryofsocialscience.com/newsletter/posts/2018/2018-04-02-final4.html

Page 84: *"a race tuberculosis"; "the ultimate goal . . ."* "Adolf Hitler Issues Comment on the 'Jewish Question.'" United States Holocaust Memorial Museum. ushmm.org/learn/timeline-of-events/before-1933/adolf-hitler-issues-comment-on-the-jewish-question

Page 84: *"non-Jewish names"* "Regulation Requiring Jews to Change Their Names." Jewish Virtual Library. jewishvirtuallibrary.org/regulation-requiring-jews-to-change-their-names

Page 85: *"un-German spirit"* "1933 Book Burnings." United States Holocaust Memorial Museum. ushmm.org/collections/bibliography/1933-book-burnings

Page 86: *"They tried to live as normally as possible . . ."* Straede, 8.

Page 88: *"As a boy . . ."* Lidegaard, 52.

Page 88: *"just another Danish girl"* Author interview with Lillan and Flemming Sundø.

Page 91: *"1. You must not . . ."* Lampe, 2–3.

Page 92: *"The occupation was on everyone's mind . . ."* Hoose, 15.

Page 93: *"If you continue . . ."* Goldberger, 79.

Page 99: *"The German invasion . . ."* Goldberger, 141.

Page 99: *"You dirty Germans . . ."* Author interview with Lillan and Flemming Sundø.

Page 101: *"A man is a man . . ."* Full text of "October 43 Aage Bertelsen." archive.org/stream/october43aageber001971mbp/october43aageber001971mbp_djvu.txt

Page 104: *"Norwegian conditions"* Lidegaard, 28.

Page 105: *"final solution"* "Reinhard Heydrich." *Encyclopaedia Britannica Online.* britannica.com/biography/Reinhard-Heydrich

Page 108: *"If the request was made . . ."* Lidegaard, xiii–ix.

Page 109: *"There [is] no Jewish question in Denmark."* Yahil, 47.

Page 109: *"As long as a Danish government . . ."* Yahil, 50.

Page 112: *"I was very upset . . ."* Kieler, *The Story of a Resistance Group.*

Page 115: *"Apart from your need . . ."* Oral History with Jørgen Kieler, 46.

Page 115: *"Only physicians . . ."* Tveskov, 79.

Page 115: *"refrain from doing . . ."* Practo. "The Hippocratic Oath: The Original and Revised Version." *The Practo Blog for Doctors,* March 10, 2015. doctors.practo.com/the-hippocratic-oath-the-original-and-revised-version/

Page 116: *"sacred and secret"* Practo. "The Hippocratic Oath: The Original and Revised Version." *The Practo Blog for Doctors,* March 10, 2015. doctors.practo.com/thehippocratic-oath-the-original-and-revised-version/

Page 118: *"We have the V . . ."* Werner, 17.

Page 119: *"Radio broadcasts . . ."* Byers, 104.

Page 120: *"This is London calling."* Hoose, 18.
Page 120: *"Jens and I . . ."* Hoose, 18.
Page 121: *"Two of us backed up our bikes . . ."* Hoose, 21.
Page 123: *"As far as propaganda was concerned . . ."* Oral History with Jørgen Kieler, 16.
Page 127: *"In Denmark there is an old castle . . ."* "A Translation of Hans Christian Andersen's 'Holger Danske' by Jean Hersholt." H.C. Andersen Centret (Hans Christian Andersen Centre). andersen.sdu.dk/vaerk/hersholt/HolgerDanske_e.html
Page 132: *"Meinen besten Dank. Chr. Rex"* Byers, 17.
Page 133: *"and the king . . . responded . . ."* Tveskov, 49.
Page 134: *"the Bloodhound of Paris"*; *"a psychopath"* Pundik, *In Denmark It Could Not Happen,* loc. 1463, Kindle.
Page 135: *"made that point of view . . ."* Author interview with Lillan and Flemming Sundø.
Page 136: *"Your family name . . ."* Author interview with Lillan and Flemming Sundø.
Page 137: *"None of us could touch-type . . ."* Kieler and Dickens, loc. 955, Kindle.
Page 138: *"What will you do if the Gestapo . . ."* Goldberger, 143.
Page 139: *"Protect him with my body . . ."* Goldberger, 143.
Page 139: *"painful"* Kieler and Dickens, loc. 1047, Kindle.
Page 139: *"Taking part in sabotage . . ."* Kieler and Dickens, loc. 1011, Kindle.
Page 140: *"criminal war"* Kieler and Dickens, loc. 1047, Kindle.
Page 146: *"We had a great time . . ."* Author interview with Lillan and Flemming Sundø.
Page 149: *"Seek Swedish waters."* Søren Nørby. "Seek Swedish Waters: The Danish Artillery Ship *Niels Juel* and the Scuttling of the Danish Navy on 29 August 1943." *Warship World* 14, no. 8 (November/December 2015): 19.
Page 150: *"Throwing the handle into the water . . ."* Author interview with Søren Nørby.
Page 152: *"ecstatic"*; *"big sorrow* and *pride"* Author interview with Flemming Sundø.
Page 154: *"I expected to be over the next morning . . ."* Kieler, *Why Did You Do It?,* 235.
Page 155: *"not fully recovered from . . . polio"*; *"At 7 [a.m.] I gave up . . ."* Kieler, *Why Did You Do It?,* 235.
Page 157: *"Curiously, [the Germans] were almost all convinced . . ."* Kieler, *Why Did You Do It?,* 235–236.
Page 157: *"immensely proud . . ."* Veisz, report I, 236.
Page 161: *"After August 29, 1943 . . ."* Memoirs of Paul Sinding.
Page 162: *"ideas of how best . . ."* Memoirs of Paul Sinding.
Page 163: *"big smile"*; *"lively eyes"*; *"keenness and impatience . . ."* Kieler and Dickens, loc. 1263, Kindle.
Page 163: *"restore Denmark's . . ."*; *"the good name . . ."* Kieler, *Why Did You Do It?,* 408.
Page 163: *"I had great confidence . . ."* Kieler and Dickens, loc. 1263, Kindle.
Page 164: *"Measures should now be taken . . ."* Yahil, 138.
Page 165: *"some 6,000 Jews . . ."* Byers, 19.
Page 166: *"his chosen fatherland"* Lidegaard, 47.
Page 169: *"We knew we had to warn . . ."* Kieler and Dickens, loc. 1559, Kindle.
Page 172: *"felt furious . . ."*; *"interfere with our Danish people . . ."* Oral History with Henny Sundø.
Page 173: *"special measures against a group of people . . ."* Levine, 72.
Page 174: *"I will assume responsibility . . ."* Werner, 36.
Page 176: *"Now the disaster is about to occur . . ."* Hans Hedtoft, foreword to *October '43.* Aage Bertelsen. Munich: Ner Tamid Verlag, 1960: 13–14.
Page 176: *"[Duckwitz's] face was white with indignation . . ."* Hedtoft, foreword to *October '43,* 13–14.
Page 177: *"I divided the job among some friends . . ."* Goldberger, 82.
Page 179: *"Some distance out to sea . . ."* Police report taken in Malmö, Sweden, October 2, 1943. Submitted to the Royal Swedish National Board of Health and Welfare, Stockholm. Courtesy of the Danish Jewish Museum.
Page 182: *"We have no time now to continue prayers . . ."* Fiona Macdonald. "The Danish Network That Defied Hitler." BBC, October 1, 2018. bbc.com/culture/article/20181001-the-danish-network-that-defied-hitler
Page 186: *"last days in September"* Oral History with Henny Sundø.

Page 187: *"The crew was gathered..."* Oral History with Henny Sundø.
Page 187: *"They said they'd been thinking..."* Oral History with Henny Sundø.
Page 189: *"If somebody comes asking you for help..."* Author interview with Lillan and Flemming Sundø.
Page 190: *"I went straight into it..."* Henny Sinding Sundø. *"Gerda III's* Efforts during World War II."
Page 191: *"Of course, Dad was okay..."* Sundø, *"Gerda III's* Efforts during World War II."
Page 191: *"Dad just looked at me..."* Marchen Jersild. "You Just Run." *Berlingske Tidende,* October 17, 1993.
Page 192: *"Already the next day..."* Oral History with Henny Sundø.
Page 192: *"The crew knew somebody..."* Sinding, *Henny's Story.*
Page 192: *"There was a door..."* Kieler, *The Story of a Resistance Group.*
Page 193: *"There was no general awareness..."* Goldberger, 83.
Page 195: *"I was home in ten minutes..."* Goldberger, 84.
Page 195: *"From one hour to the next..."* Hopkinson, 150.
Page 196: *"three completely spontaneous visits..."* Sofie Lene Bak. "Copenhagen: Bright Hope and Deep Gloom—a New View of the 1943 Rescue Operation in Denmark." In *Civil Society and the Holocaust: International Perspectives on Resistance and Rescue,* Anders Jerichow and Cecilie Felicia Stokholm Banke, eds., 18–39. New York: Humanity in Action Press, 2013. humanityinaction.org/knowledge_detail/copenhagen-bright-hope-and-deep-gloom-a-new-view-of-the-1943-rescue-operation-in-denmark/
Page 197: *"If there is room in your heart..."* Author interview with Malene Sølvdahl Clementsen.
Page 197: *"It was exactly the same..."* "Danish Citizens Who Saved Jews in Denmark." Rescue in the Holocaust. holocaustrescue.org/danish-citizens
Page 197: *"It was my duty as a Dane..."* Oral History with Mogens Staffeldt.
Page 198: *"I would have done it for anybody..."* Donald Harrison. "'Girl in Red Cap' Saved Hundreds of Jews." *San Diego Jewish Press-Heritage,* January 14, 1994. sandiegojewishworld.com/denmark/copenhagen/1994-01-14_red_cap_girl.htm
Page 198: *"I felt it had to be done..."* "Danish Citizens."
Page 198: *"All decent people did..."* "Danish Citizens"; Flender, 138–139.
Page 198: *"The Germans' picking on Jews..."* "Danish Citizens"; Flender, 124; Byers, 36.
Page 198: *"We were not heroes..."* Letter from Henny Sinding to Faye and Mike Lieman. October 20, 1997. Dragør Local Archives.
Page 205: *"I have six tons of potatoes..."* Werner, 46.
Page 206: *"To our chagrin..."* Goldberger, 162.
Page 208: *"It was terrible to see..."* Werner, 104.
Page 215: *"the Jews have been removed..."* Levine, 72.
Page 215: *"At least forty protests..."* Yahil, 231.
Page 216: *"Every man has a value in the eyes of God..."* Goldberger, 6–7.
Page 216: *"The result was meager..."* Lidegaard, 198.
Page 217: *"Father and Mother never said anything..."* Kieler, *The Story of a Resistance Group.*
Page 218: *"I knew a lot of Jews..."* Oral History with Henny Sundø.
Page 219: *"Just one wrong person's knowledge..."* Kieler, *The Story of a Resistance Group.*
Page 220: *"As soon as you got hold of one or two..."* Oral History with Henny Sundø.
Page 221: *"Prices per person varied..."* Goldberger, 91.
Page 221: *"the monthly salary for a fully trained worker..."* Lene Bak, "Copenhagen."
Page 222: *"The wealthier of the refugees..."*; *"were paid with a bottle of Snaps..."* Munkholt, "Ellen Wilhelmine Nielsen, née Lundquist's Help in October 1943 to Jewish Refugees Fleeing to Sweden via Dragør, Denmark." dragoerhistorie.dk/wp-content/uploads/2017/01/Ellen-Wilhelmine-Nielsen-help-to-jewish-refugees.pdf
Page 224: *"A Small Dunkirk"* Straede, 21.
Page 224: *"We did not think too much about any risk..."* Author interview with Flemming Sundø.
Page 225: *"If German patrol boats turned up..."* Hopkinson, 164.
Page 228: *"[when] the official message..."* Kieler, *The Story of a Resistance Group.*
Page 228: *"[The] long discussions in our apartment..."*; *"We got together in our little apartment..."* Oral History with Jørgen Kieler, 33.
Page 229: *"The financial problems were solved..."* Goldberger, 146.

Page 230: *"She knew all the fishermen . . ."* Oral History with Jørgen Kieler, 41.

Page 231: *"[Our] main problem . . ."* Oral History with Jørgen Kieler, 41.

Page 233: *"the first people I arranged transport for . . ."* Kieler and Dickens, loc. 1684, Kindle.

Page 233: *"A hectic time started . . ."* Oral History with Henny Sundø.

Page 234: *"Getting into the Resistance movement . . ."* Oral History with Henny Sundø.

Page 235: *"Do you know a girl . . ."* Oral History with Henny Sundø.

Page 236: *"Mix looked me up one day . . ."*; *"For a long time we walked and talked . . ."* Oral History with Henny Sundø.

Page 237: *"[She] had been active with the transports . . ."* Kieler and Dickens, loc. 2055, Kindle.

Page 237: *"Through their personal contacts . . ."* Goldberger, 146.

Page 239: *"For the next fourteen days . . ."* Oral History with Mogens Staffeldt.

Page 240: *"Word by word . . ."* Oral History with Jørgen Kieler, 42.

Page 241: *"We had to divide them into teams . . ."* Sundø, *Henny's Story.*

Page 242: *"You had to do it in daytime . . ."*; *"I always paid half . . ."* Oral History with Ebba Lund.

Page 242: *"October was peak season for herring . . ."* Straede, 19.

Page 243: *"It was completely crazy . . ."*; *"It was exhilarating!"* Sundø, *Henny's Story.*

Page 250: *"Sometimes he would go to the window . . ."*; *"The Germans are coming!"*; *"Ah, stop that nonsense"*; *"True enough . . ."* Interview with Aron Engelhardt, 42–43.

Page 251: *"We better open the door . . ."*; *"I was too afraid to open the door . . ."* Interview with Aron Engelhardt, 42–43.

Page 252: *"We were dropped off . . ."* Interview with Aron Engelhardt, 43.

Page 253: *"We were told that we would be going . . ."* Interview with Aron Engelhardt, 43.

Page 255: *"It drove through the city . . ."* Interview with Aron Engelhardt, 43.

Page 256: *"Incredibly, we were lucky enough . . ."* Interview with Aron Engelhardt, 43.

Page 257: *"There was always something to eat . . ."* Interview with Aron Engelhardt, 43.

Page 258: *"It was nervewrecking . . ."*

Page 258: *"When all the adults were onboard . . ."* Kieler, *The Story of a Resistance Group.*

Page 259: *"One by one . . ."* Veisz, *Henny's Boat: The Maritime Rescue Operation that Saved Denmark's Jews and Sparked a Nationwide Revolt Against the Nazis.*

Page 260: *"We all said a silent prayer . . ."* Kieler, *The Story of a Resistance Group.*

Page 260: *"the tramp of boots on the deck . . ."* Veisz, 63.

Page 260: *"Either they were nice Germans . . ."* Kieler, *The Story of a Resistance Group.*

Page 261: *"This is how* Gerda III *was sneaked to the sea . . ."* Kieler, *The Story of a Resistance Group.*

Page 263: *"the lighthouse cutter . . ."* Kieler, *The Story of a Resistance Group.*

Page 263: *"under the Knippelsbro Bridge . . ."*; *"Germans soldiers patrolling the bridges"* Veisz, 72–73.

Page 264: *"I stood in the warehouse . . ."* Kieler, *The Story of a Resistance Group.*

Page 269: *"They [listened] to the tick-tock . . ."* Leif Holmstrøm, 2008 parish priest of Gilleleje Church, in "Permanent Exhibition—Danish Rescue Boat." Holocaust Museum Houston. YouTube, October 10, 2013. youtube.com/watch?v=0O7mGv6l4ao

Page 270: *"a sight that made him hold his breath . . ."* Flender, loc. 4636, Kindle.

Page 271: *"Not me . . ."* Flender, loc. 4636, Kindle.

Page 271: *"I tried getting to the roof . . ."* Jersild, "You Just Run."

Page 272: *"more dead than alive"* Lidegaard, 289.

Page 274: *"I ran away from there . . ."* Jersild, "You Just Run."

Page 275: *"In a situation like that . . ."* Jersild, "You Just Run."

Page 00: *"I darted across the quay . . ."*; *"an eternity"*; *"I was lying in the cargo . . ."* Jersild, "You Just Run."

Page 277: *"Someone opened the hatch and said . . ."* Jersild, "You Just Run."

Page 277: *"every night, many weeks in a row"* Kieler, *The Story of a Resistance Group.*

Page 279: *"their fiction of a peaceful occupation"*; *"After the mass raids . . ."* Lene Bak, "Copenhagen."

Page 280: *"rooting out Danish spies . . ."* Lene Bak, "Copenhagen."

Page 281: *"The German captain shouted . . ."* Ulrich Plesner, letter, *Jerusalem Post*, January 30, 1979.

Page 282: *"We are standing on the beach . . ."* Goldberger, 93.

Page 283: *"The Danes saved the Jews . . ."* Goldberger, 94.

Page 284: *"Few boats, if any . . ."* Veisz, v.

Page 286: *"The dark night of the first and second of October . . ."* Aage Bertelsen. *October 43.*

New York: Putnam, 1954: 24. archive.org/stream/october43aageber001971mbp/
october43aageber001971mbp_djvu.txt

Page 286: *"It took a long time . . ."* Yahil, 248.

Page 290: *"On October 14 . . ."* Kieler and Dickens, loc. 2055, Kindle.

Page 290: *"sabotage was considered a man's job"* Hopkinson, 188; Kieler and Dickens, loc. 2083, Kindle.

Page 290: *"included four women . . ."* Kieler, *Resistance Fighter*, loc. 2092.

Page 291: *"It was necessary . . ."* Halter, 130.

Page 293: *"I usually walked with one of the boys . . ."* Oral History with Henny Sundø.

Page 294: *"they acted as [a] couple . . ."* Birkelund, 190.

Page 294: *"He was much loved by his comrades . . ."* Kieler, *Why Did You Do It?*, 408.

Page 295: *"illegal activities"*; *"something"* Author interview with Flemming Sundø.

Page 296: *"What better cover could we get!"* Author interview with Flemming Sundø.

Page 298: *"When we went into action . . ."* Kieler, *Why Did You Do It?*, 328.

Page 299: *"You have two minutes . . ."* Oral History with Jørgen Kieler, 36.

Page 299: *"[the cadets] agreed . . ."* Kieler, *Why Did You Do It?*, 407.

Page 300: *"They had found that Mix . . ."* Kieler, *Why Did You Do It?*, 407.

Page 301: *"Everything went wrong."* Oral History with Henny Sundø.

Page 302: *"Play for time . . ."* Kieler and Dickens, loc. 3062, Kindle.

Page 302: *"I should have been dead scared . . ."* Sundø, *Henny's Story*, 32.

Page 303: *"It was too risky . . ."* Veisz, 107–8.

Page 306: *"[It was] much against my will . . ."* Sundø, *Henny's Story*, 10.

Page 306: *"I was pretty mad . . ."*; *"So . . . we all had to obey orders . . ."* Kieler, *The Story of a Resistance Group*, 253.

Page 307: *"In the prison, they had . . ."* Oral History with Henny Sundø.

Page 308: *"There was no way around it . . ."*; *"Mum was just as fantastic . . ."* Kieler, *The Story of a Resistance Group*, 254.

Page 309: *"Mix . . . borrowed an apartment . . ."* Kieler, *The Story of a Resistance Group*, 254.

Page 309: *"Luckily, Mix and I were in touch . . ."* Kieler, *The Story of a Resistance Group*, 255.

Page 310: *"[He] said that there was someone . . ."* Kieler, *The Story of a Resistance Group*, 255.

Page 311: *"We never saw [Mogens's brother] . . ."* Kieler, *The Story of a Resistance Group*, 255.

Page 311: *"That same evening Mix and I . . ."* Kieler, *The Story of a Resistance Group*, 256.

Page 312: *"It was not until late . . ."* Kieler, *The Story of a Resistance Group*, 264.

Page 313: *"The motorboat simply could not dock . . ."*; *"The next evening . . ."* Kieler, *The Story of a Resistance Group*, 264.

Page 313: *"We were . . . out into the Øresund . . ."* Kieler, *The Story of a Resistance Group*, 265.

Page 316: *"If the flywheel of the engine . . ."* Kieler, *The Story of a Resistance Group*, 265.

Page 318: *"We were taken to some 'spa town' . . ."* Kieler, *The Story of a Resistance Group*, 265.

Page 319: *"It was a strange feeling . . ."* Kieler, *The Story of a Resistance Group*, 266.

Page 320: *"We were not very well received . . ."* Sundø, *Henny's Story*, 13.

Page 321: *"an old hovel . . ."*; *"she knew nothing . . ."* Sundø, *Henny's Story*, 13.

Page 321: *"I'd rather be out in the field . . ."* Sundø, *Henny's Story*, 16.

Page 321: *"In between, there were many tears . . ."* Sundø, *Henny's Story*, 17.

Page 323: *"with Mix and the boys"*; *"Mix was determined that we should get married."* Veisz, 122.

Page 323: *"I felt the future was so insecure . . ."* Kieler, *The Story of a Resistance Group*, 192.

Page 324: *"Mix has left."* Kieler, *The Story of a Resistance Group*, 192.

Page 325: *"The role of a passive observer was not for Mix."* Kieler and Dickens, loc. 5050, Kindle.

Page 325: *"just as confused"*; *"I was full of admiration . . ."* Kieler, *The Story of a Resistance Group*, 195.

Page 326: *"illegal work"*; *"multiples of times . . ."* Memoirs of Paul Sinding.

Page 327: *"[At four a.m.,] the Germans . . ."* Kieler, *The Story of a Resistance Group*, 192.

Page 328: *"The Gestapo . . ."* Memoirs of Paul Sinding.

Page 329: *"Both my wife and I went into hiding . . ."*; *"Someone had seen a Gestapo car . . ."* Memoirs of Paul Sinding.

Page 331: *"Being here is a little like driving along a cliff . . ."* Kieler, *The Story of a Resistance Group*, 198.

Page 331: *"greatest achievement"* Goldberger, 148.

Page 331: *"particular credit"* Goldberger, 154.

Page 332: *"My team had a terrible disappointment . . ."* Letter from Mix to Henny, February 23, 1945, in Veisz, 124.

Page 334: *"We had our time and it will come again . . ."*; *"dynamic navy cadet"* Veisz, 124.

Page 336: *"And then we heard the BBC . . ."* Oral History with Henny Sundø.

Page 336: *"All German forces . . ."* Levine, 140.

Page 337: *"It may sound strange . . ."* Sundø, *Henny's Story*, 24.

Page 337: *"The thought that we didn't get to . . ."* Sundø, *Henny's Story*, 26.

Page 338: *"And everywhere, we drove through Sweden . . ."* Oral History with Henny Sundø.

Page 340: *"Suddenly I felt someone pushing me . . ."* Oral History with Henny Sundø.

Page 341: *"There were many, many people with flags . . ."* Oral History with Henny Sundø.

Page 341: *"rotten in the state of Denmark"*; *"words, words, words"*; *"to thine own self be true"* William Shakespeare. *Hamlet.* New York: Simon & Schuster, 1992.

Page 344: *"climbed to the summit . . ."* Wiesel, foreword to *The Courage to Care: Rescuers of Jews During the Holocaust*, xi.

Page 347: *"I don't think a day goes by . . ."* Sundø, *Henny's Story*, 32.

Page 348: *"Myself included . . ."* Oral History with Henny Sundø.

Page 348: *"I have never expected a thank-you . . ."* Jersild, "You Just Run"; author interview with Flemming Sundø.

Page 352: *"Thank you for my life."* Jersild, "You Just Run"; author interview with Flemming Sundø.

Page 354: *"About 99 percent of the Jews in Denmark survived . . ."* Herbert Pundik, "The Anonymous," *Politiken*, October 3, 1993.

Page 355: *"Many reports are unspecific . . ."* Author interview with Therkel Straede.

Page 356: *"every Dane who [helps] the Germans . . ."* "Danish Organizations That Aided Jews." Rescue in the Holocaust. holocaustrescue.org/danish-organizations

Page 356: *"15,000 were arrested; 13,521 found guilty . . ."* Levine, 145.

Page 357: *"The reality of what Denmark did . . ."* Meyer Lieman, speech at ceremony to honor Righteous Gentiles in Denmark, August 26, 1997.

Page 357: *"I have never expected a thank-you . . ."* Jersild, "You Just Run."

Page 357: *"I am rather embarrassed . . ."* Letter from Henny Sinding to Faye and Mike Lieman.

WITH GRATITUDE

I am indebted to so many people for their expertise, advice, and gracious patience as I wrote this book. First, thank you to Howard Veisz, for caring for *Gerda III* at the Mystic Seaport Museum; for your adult book *Henny's Boat: The Maritime Rescue Operation that Saved Denmark's Jews and Sparked a Nationwide Revolt Against the Nazis*; for your support of a children's book about this amazing woman; and for putting me in touch with Henny's family in Denmark. Mange tak to Henny Sinding Sundø's daughter Lillan, and nephew Flemming Sundø, along with Flemming's wife, Marielle Sundø, and his brothers Carsten and Ole, for answering my endless questions and for escorting me around Denmark.

Flemming organized a jam-packed, fascinating itinerary, allowing me to see where Henny grew up and went to school, where she learned to sail at Hellerup Havn, where she worked with the Lighthouse and Buoy Service, where *Gerda III* was berthed outside of Hans Just's warehouse. I visited the Naval Cadet School on Holmen, Jørgen Kieler's apartment building, Nazi headquarters, the site of Mogens Staffeldt's bookstore, the street where Mix was shot and the grave where he is buried. We attended the somber, moving May 4 ceremony at Ryvangen Memorial Park, annually commemorating those in the Resistance who died for their country. Flemming also arranged for expert tours: with Marielle Sundø in Copenhagen; with Helle Vibeke Bjorholm, who showed us the fishing village of Dragør and arranged a special trip aboard *Gerda IV* to Drogden Lighthouse; with Carsten Sundø, who showed us the fishing boats' points of departure all along the coast; and with Tove Udsholt, who shared her childhood experiences as a Jewish refugee in Gilleleje.

On this trip, Flemming helped me find Sigurd Lilienfeldt, who shared photos of his dad, Gerd; and Kirsten Tønnesen, who sent me photos of her grandfather—*Gerda III* captain Ejnar Tønnesen. In the course of a week, I found Henny's nephew could orchestrate just about anything—including a spur-of-the-moment tour of Henny's house! I'm indebted to your curiosity, ingenuity, and generous good cheer.

I couldn't have written this book without my Danish researchers and translators Malene Sølvdahl Clementsen and Sarah Vestergaard Andersen. They spent months tracking down leads and unearthing archives.

Museum staff in America and Denmark assisted in uncovering facts and photos. I'm indebted to Jack Kliger, Joshua Mack, Treva Walsh, Maggie Radd, Elizabeth Edelstein, Ellen Bari, and Haley Coopersmith at the Museum of Jewish Heritage—A Living Memorial to the Holocaust, in New York. I'm also grateful to the maritime staff of Mystic Seaport Museum who take care of *Gerda III*, ensuring many generations will know her amazing history.

In Denmark, thanks to Bo Braestrup, who conducted ground-breaking research to determine *Gerda III*'s exact berth when moved from Holmen. Thanks, also, to Dr. Benjamin Asmussen of the Maritime Museum of Denmark; Julie Avery and Peter Birkelund at the Danish National Archives; to Janus Møller Jensen, Sara Fredfeldt Stadager, and Signe Bergman Larsen at the Danish Jewish Museum; to Søren Mentz at the Museum Amager; and to Julie Lorenzen at the Danish War Museum and the Museum of Danish Resistance.

I'm also grateful for the work of three historians: Dr. Sofie Lene Bak at the University of Copenhagen, Dr. Søren Nørby of the Royal Danish Defence College, and Dr. Therkel Straede of the University of Southern Denmark. They helped me gain a fuller understanding of the flight of the Danish Jews from a modern perspective.

Thank you to Lois Lowry for writing *Number the Stars*, an all-time favorite book that first introduced me to the flight of the Danish Jews years ago. Much gratitude to my writers' group, especially to Susan Montanari for reading an early draft.

I thank my lucky stars every day that I get to make books with my beloved agent, Brenda Bowen, and my brilliant editors Nancy Inteli and Megan Ilnitzki. Thank you for your smarts and all the tender loving care you take with my manuscripts. Cheers to the whole team at HarperCollins—Erika DiPasquale, Kathryn Silsand, Megan Gendell, Andrea Vandergrift, Joel Tippie, Kristen Eckhardt, Samantha Brown, Patty Rosati, Rosanne Lauer, and Susan Bishansky.

Love and thanks to my daughters, Allison and Emily, for listening and to my husband, Paul Kueffner, for your nautical expertise, your endless interest and undying support of my work, and your willingness to read the book aloud to me, more than once!